Natural
Ther
to Ad
Fatigue
Syndrome

Proper Use of Vitamins, Glandulars, Herbs and Hormones

Michael Lam, M.D., M.P.H.

Dorine Lam, R.D., M.S., M.P.H.

Natural Therapeutics to Adrenal Fatigue Syndrome:
Proper Use of Vitamins, Glandulars, Herbs and Hormones
by Michael Lam, M.D., M.P.H. and Dorine Lam, R.D., M.S., M.P.H.

Published in the United States by:

Adrenal Institute Press, Loma Linda, CA 92354
www.AdrenalInstitute.org

Cover and Interior Design: Nick Zelinger, NZ Graphics
Editing: John Maling (Editing By John), Virginia McCullough
Book Shepherding: Judith Briles

The authors of this book do not dispense medical advice or prescribe the use of any technique or natural compounds as forms of prevention and treatment for physical, emotional, or medical programs without the advice of a physician, either directly or indirectly. The intent of the authors is only to offer information of a general nature to help you in your quest for well-being. This book is not meant to replace the advice and treatments prescribed by your healthcare provider. It is not meant to encourage treatment of any illness by the layman. In the event you use any of the information in this book for yourself, which is your right, you assume risk, and the authors and the publishers assume no responsibilities for your actions. If you are under a physician's care for any condition, he or she can advise you about information described in this book. The authors or publisher shall have neither liability for nor responsibility to any person or entity with respect to any loss, damage, injury caused or alleged to be caused directly or indirectly by the information contained in this book.

Any trademarks, service marks, product names, or named features are assumed to be the property of their respective owners, and are used only for reference. There is no implied endorsement if we use one of these terms.

ISBN (paperback): 978-1-937930-07-3
ISBN (ebook): 978-1-937930-08-0
Library of Congress Control Number: 2012936506

Natural Therapeutics to Adrenal Fatigue Syndrome: Proper Use of Vitamins, Glandulars, Herbs and Hormones / Michael Lam, Dorine Lam. First edition, 2012

10 9 8 7 6 5 4 3 2 1

1. Health 2. Adrenal glands—Disease. 3. Fatigue 4. Stress (Physiology) 5. Neuroendocrine

First Edition

Printed in the United States of America

Contents

Author's Note

When you experience chronic stress—physically or emotionally—your adrenal glands can become overworked and burdened. Adrenal Fatigue Syndrome has entered your life. Your body needs, demands, a carefully designed nutritional program to not only start your recovery, but to keep you on track for the rest of your life.

Recovery from AFS requires a carefully designed program of nutritional therapeutics. Wrong or inappropriate use of nutrients is a common recovery program error.

Don't be mislead—not all nutritional supplements and therapeutics are the same. Gentle, nurturing and non-stimulating, natural compounds are best.

Natural Therapeutics and Adrenal Fatigue Syndrome: Proper Use of Vitamins, Glandulars, Herbs and Hormones will go into great detail on the most common nutritional tools available to suffers of Adrenal Fatigue, presented in order of potency. Knowing how and when to use each will facilitate your recovery.

Dr. Lam

Note: This book is part of Dr. Lam's Adrenal Recovery Series™ and all information can be found in *Adrenal Fatigue Syndrome: Reclaim Your Energy and Vitality with Clinically Proven Natural Programs.*

Introduction

Fatigue and lethargy are two of the most common complaints doctors hear from their adult patients, both of which are symptoms of a silent epidemic condition known as Adrenal Fatigue Syndrome (AFS). This condition is as old as humankind, but its incidence has skyrocketed as our society and our lifestyles have become increasingly complex and high-pressured.

From a sufferer's point of view, Adrenal Fatigue Syndrome is confusing and frustrating. We can see the everyday consequences of Adrenal Fatigue Syndrome in the following statements:

- I'm tired all the time—I manage to keep going on my job, but I drink coffee every few hours to get through
- I used to merely gripe and complain about feeling tired, but now the fatigue is so overwhelming and debilitating, I'm underperforming on my job.
- I'm anxious and fearful much of the time.
- I seem to catch every cold or flu that comes around.
- My joints ache, and my doctor said I probably have arthritis, even though I just turned 40.
- I'm depressed and can't think straight—I feel like I walk around with brain fog.
- I've tried every diet in the book, but I can't lose weight.
- I wake up at 3:00 AM and toss and turn for hours and cannot fall asleep again.
- I used to have great energy, but now a short walk wears me out.

These statements personalize some of the typical—and persistent—signs and symptoms of Adrenal Fatigue Syndrome. You might have described these same things to your doctor, or you may have noted these changes in your health or know someone who has these complaints, but you don't know what to make of them. If you're over age forty-five or fifty, you might even be told to attribute your symptoms to "normal" aging!

Below, you'll find an expanded list of the signs and symptoms of Adrenal Fatigue Syndrome. Not surprisingly, many of these symptoms are also related to other conditions, and they match the statements listed above:

- Often feels tired between 9:00 and 10:00 PM, but resists going to bed
- Difficulty getting out of bed in the morning
- Cravings for salty, fatty, and high protein food such as meat and cheese
- For women, increased symptoms of PMS and irregular menstrual bleeding, with days of heavy flow that stops (or nearly stops) on day 4, only to resume on days 5 or 6 of the menstrual cycle
- Pain in the upper back or neck with no apparent reason
- Tendency to feel better on vacation and when stress is relieved
- Food and or inhalant (air borne) allergies
- Dry and thin skin
- Hypoglycemia but blood sugar is normal
- Low body temperature despite thyroid medication

- Heart palpitations when heart is normal
- Unexplained hair loss
- Recurrent miscarriages in the first trimester
- Low blood pressure, dizziness, and vertigo

As you can see, Adrenal Fatigue Syndrome has a broad spectrum of symptoms, many of which seem nonspecific, and, therefore, are often reframed as psychological in origin, such as anxiety or depression. Sometimes patients are told that these symptoms are "nothing that some rest won't cure." However, it is clear that Adrenal Fatigue Syndrome is not that simple. Research shows that AFS at its core represents the body's neuroendocrine stress response when under threat.

Do not confuse AFS with Addison's disease.

Addison's disease is often caused by an autoimmune dysfunction, whereas stress and a host of other factors are the primary culprits of Adrenal Fatigue Syndrome. The symptoms of Addison's disease include low energy, joint and abdominal pain, weight loss, diarrhea, fever, and electrolyte imbalances. Some AFS sufferers report these symptoms too, but they are usually much less intense.

Both lead to low cortisol output in the adrenal glands, though those with AFS can be symptomatic despite the fact that laboratory tests are usually normal. Currently, conventional medicine recognizes only Addison's disease as a legitimate disease of low adrenal function. If, for example, you ask your doctor if your symptoms could point to Adrenal Fatigue Syndrome, you may learn that he or she has not heard of AFS or may deny its existence.

Adrenal Fatigue Syndrome (AFS) consists of four broad and overlapping clinical stages, from mild to severe. Stages 1 (Alarm

Reaction) and 2 (Resistance Response) are generally mild. Some fatigue is present, but not debilitating. Few are alerted and seek professional help. By the time Stage 3 (Adrenal Exhaustion) arrives, most have seen their physician for lack of energy and are usually told all is well after an extensive workup. Fatigue in Stage 4 (Adrenal Failure) is severe and most sufferers are bedridden.

Chapter 1

Nutritional Supplements for Adrenal Fatigue: An Introduction

When correctly used, nutritional supplements play a large role in adrenal support and recovery. In particular, they help to provide the necessary ingredients for the adrenals to produce the hormones required. They help to stabilize HPA axis dysregulation, rebalance the autonomic nervous system, enhance brain function, and reduce inflammation, just to name a few.

Consider the following:

- Vitamins C and B provide the necessary raw material for the adrenal glands to make a wide variety of hormones that may be deficient.
- Vitamins A and D are generally anti-inflammatory.
- Omega 3 vs. omega 6 balance helps determine the balance between inflammation and anti-inflammation.
- Vitamin D reduces insulin resistance which helps the body tolerate low blood sugar from cortisol dysregulation.
- Vitamin D increases serotonin and dopamine production.
- B vitamins are necessary cofactors for many of the processes involved in neurotransmitter signaling.

- Magnesium is a necessary cofactor in many enzymatic reactions.
- Glandulars and herbal compounds can help provide additional support when the adrenals are weak, while calming the adrenals when they are in overdrive. Hormonal therapies have their place, too, especially in times of acute stress.

Nutrient Recovery Toolbox

We can look at these three general categories of recovery tools on a continuum of potency:

- Vitamins, enzymes, probiotics, and minerals are generally the gentlest tools in the toolbox.
- Glandulars and herbal compounds tend to be mildly potent.
- Hormonal medications tend to be the most potent and, if not properly used, often produce undesirable side effects and potential addiction problems.

This broad classification provides only general rules. For specific outcomes, we need to look at the form, delivery system, and dosage of each. In that respect, the above categories are designed to give us a bird's eye view rather than a specific protocol. The following examples will clarify what we mean:

- High dose vitamin B5 (pantothenic acid) is more potent then low dose pantethine (explained in the next chapter) within the vitamin B category.
- Low dose hormones can be less potent than certain forms of glandular compounds when the body is sensitive.

- Sublingual vitamin B12 is a far more potent form than its capsule form.
- A cream form of natural progesterone is far gentler for the liver than oral forms of progesterone (called Prometrium®).

Using the right nutritional cocktail of vitamins, minerals, glandulars, and herbs at the right time can often be equally or more effective than using prescription steroids.

We tend to gauge supplements by their potency to help us compartmentalize them in our mind, but potency in and of itself should not be the sole yardstick used when evaluating and choosing the right supplements. One can easily bring about a higher level of energy with more potent supplements, but the energy coming from that strategy is often not natural. In other words, the person may feel a sense of being propped up, but that could bring with it a sense of anxiety. As a result, one can be energized and feel tired at the same time, which we've previously described as feeling artificially wired-and-tired, a classic sign of energizing the body in the wrong way. It's a misleading situation.

A short term boost can often result in a longer term crash when the body finally rejects such ill fated attempts to heal the adrenals with compounds unwelcome by it. We can't forget that the body always wins these battles.

Caveats exist for the subjective classification we've designed for educational purposes. We don't want them to be taken literally as part of a structured protocol. Unfortunately, no one can offer a perfect cookbook supplement program because each person is unique. Most individuals with Adrenal Fatigue Syndrome do better with a well designed cocktail of supplements, but some do better with single supplements. As we've said, paradoxical reactions occur, and in extreme cases, supplements may be contraindicated.

The best supplement programs match the individual needs with the characteristics of each compound, and usually use the best of each class as needed, along with various forms and delivery systems. The proper blend of supplements facilitates the body's absorption capacity to match clearance capability, meaning that unwanted metabolites are excreted out of the body on a timely basis, thus avoiding toxic built up.

The key to selecting the right supplement cocktail involves thorough knowledge of the unique properties and effects of each compound, along with the individual's detailed nutritional history. Each person is different in terms of constitution, body sensitivity, stage of adrenal weakness, and reaction, so a nutrient beneficial to one person can be toxic to another. Even in the best of hands, some trial and error is required.

Natural compounds have a variety of properties to keep in mind:

- First, the way many natural compounds behave at one dose can be very different from how they behave at another dose.

- Second, what is considered an optimal dose is not well known or established. The RDA (Recommended Dietary Allowance) was set up for vitamins and minerals (primarily) as a guide to prevent recognized vitamin deficiency diseases such as scurvy or rickets. The prevailing view among many in holistic and nutritional medicine is that the RDAs for many vitamins and minerals are insufficient to maintain optimum health, and are irrelevant to the concept of therapeutic uses.

- Third, most natural compounds have few or no recognizable side effects at doses many times higher than the RDA, because the body has a built in mechanism to metabolize them effectively.

- Fourth, we have few studies about possible toxic consequences of many of the natural compounds at high doses, primarily because it's difficult to fund studies on non-patentable natural compounds. As a result, we lack standardization of these compounds.

- Fifth, the same natural compounds (such as certain herbs) have adaptogenic properties. This means they can behave differently in the same person, depending on that person's state of dysfunction. The same compound can be beneficial to those with mild AFS, but can become stimulatory when the fatigue is severe.

- Sixth, the optimum therapeutic dosage required for recovery is body specific. The right dosage for one person can be very different for another person, even if the degree of adrenal weakness is similar.

- Seventh, depending on the delivery system, we see a drastic difference in the bioavailability of nutrients to the cells. For example, the absorption rate of high dose orally delivered vitamin C by capsule or powder is far less than that achieved with the liposomalized form (discussed in the next chapter and in Appendix C).
- Eighth, manufacturers of natural compounds use different grades and purities, but this is not disclosed to the consumer on the bottle labels. Low quality nutritional supplements are usually less effective than higher quality supplements.

Nutritional supplements are widely used by consumers, but because the average consumer doesn't know much about them in detail, they often misuse these products. In addition, incompletely informed consumers don't know what compound to take, how much of it, or what form to use. It is no surprise that therapeutic failure is common.

When natural compounds are used inappropriately, recovery is not only impeded, but the condition often worsens over time. In these situations the compounds do more harm than good. This is one of the most common mistakes made among those who embark on self guided and nonprofessionally guided programs, especially if the Adrenal Fatigue Syndrome is advanced. Therefore, it is impossible to provide anything but general guidelines about nutritional supplements, leaving the precise dosage, delivery system, form, and the ultimate cocktail to a qualified healthcare practitioner.

Why We Recommend a Nutritional Cocktail

Through the years we have found that a well structured nutritional cocktail promotes AFS recovery far better than any other approach. This is why:

- First, different nutrients work at different parts of the cell. Vitamin C, for example, is water soluble and protects us from free radical attacks outside the cell. Vitamin E, on the other hand, is fat soluble. It is able to penetrate the cell wall easily and combat oxidative damage intracellularly.
- Second, different nutrients complement each other in their duties. Numerous studies have shown that taking multiple nutrients in their optimal dosages is better than taking single vitamins. No magic bullet exists in nutritional supplementation. It is wise to obtain broad coverage. Glutathione, for example, complements vitamin C, and vice versa.
- Third, different nutrients have different target organs. For example, saw palmetto focuses on the prostate gland, while milk thistle focuses on the liver, gingko has blood thinning properties, and vitamin E improves circulation to the brain.
- Fourth, by combining the synergistic effects of multiple nutrients, the dosage of any single nutrient is decreased. It has been shown, for example, that the oxidative effect of a combination of vitamins C, A, and E is much higher than when any one of these vitamins is used alone to achieve the same effect.

In the next three chapters, we introduce some of the tools we use. We have organized them to closely match how they are used in our daily practice, reflecting the clinical approach we take by using the gentlest nutrients as the first line of defense.

Group 1: First Line of Defense

Key compounds in this group include vitamins C, D, E, B12, B6, B5, magnesium, digestive enzymes, iodine, glutathione, lecithin, NADH, inosital, pantethine/pantothenic acid, D-ribose, collagen, fish oil, and CoQ10, just to mention a few. We have found that even with advanced Adrenal Fatigue Syndrome, these nutrients are of great benefit. Not all are needed at the same time. In fact, most of the time, we use only a select few. The key is using the *right* tools. Even a damaged body can heal if we only give it the right tools with the right delivery system at the right time. Indeed, we are saddened when sufferers come to us with a long list of potent supplements (sometimes twenty or more). They can't stop taking them because many have potential unpleasant withdrawal symptoms, but they can't continue them either because they are wired-and-tired. Before one embarks on any nutritional program, the exit strategy must be considered.

When properly combined, this group of gentle compounds facilitates a smooth recovery process, including a sense of calm and natural revitalization with few withdrawal or addiction issues when the time comes to discontinue.

Sometimes, however, this group may not be enough. In such cases, we can consider and slowly move our way up to Group 2 as needed.

Group 2: Used Only as Needed and with Great Care

The second group of compounds, glandulars and herbs, are considered more potent than those in Group 1. Again, this is a rule of thumb only. Ultimate clinical efficacy depends very much on dosage, delivery system, and the body's acceptance. This group includes adrenal and thyroid glandulars, licorice, rhodiola rosea, maca root, ashawandgha, and ginseng. These have good adrenal adaptogenic properties and are particularly suited for mild Adrenal Fatigue Syndrome.

As a general rule, they also tend to be increasingly stimulatory as adrenal weakness progresses. This is, however, not universally true. Those with advanced Adrenal Fatigue Syndrome (Stage 3 and beyond) should exercise great care. Many individuals have a false sense of complacency after starting these compounds because they feel energized. Unfortunately, in the long run they find themselves addicted and unable to stop taking them, or they may need increasingly larger doses to maintain the same energy. Invariably, the dosage eventually reaches the maximum stimulatory level and devastating crashes follow.

Group 3: Used As a Last Resort

This last group consists of hormones, including prohormones such as pregnenolone, weak hormones such as DHEA, and strong hormones such as testosterone and hydrocortisone. Hormones are the ultimate chemical messengers that control the body. While useful in managing acute AFS in a crisis situation, we're sad to see so many individuals on long term steroid use and unable to get off.

As you have surmised, our philosophy is to use the gentlest compounds possible, moving to more potent nutrients when all less potent avenues have been exhausted. The reason is simple: The higher the potency, the more side effects, and the harder it is to discontinue due to addiction and withdrawal problems.

Once adrenal function normalizes, nutritional supplements should be reduced or eliminated. As mentioned before, we are always mindful to keep this important exit strategy in mind as we design the right protocol, because we want the body ultimately to be on its own, and if possible, without dependence on any external support.

Where to Buy Supplements?

As you can see, the nutritional toolbox for AFS easily contains hundreds of natural compounds. Each has its place. The task of selecting the proper nutrients, dosage, and delivery system is a clinical art that takes decades to master. Because wrong nutrients can actually makes matter worse, we recommend seeking professional help, especially if you are in the advance stages of Adrenal Fatigue Syndrome. Those, however, who are in early stages, or those who are healthy and wishing to prevent AFS, have more latitude and self-navigation is acceptable.

From our experience, nutritional cocktail blends work the best because most nutrients work synergistically and potentially affect each other when properly compounded. Furthermore, with the blends, one can reduce the number of nutrients needed. Remember that more is not necessarily better in AFS. See Appendix G for the specific line of supplements we recommend.

Key Points to Remember

- Nutritional supplements are generally very important and useful in Adrenal Fatigue Syndrome recovery.
- The proper characteristic, dosage, form, delivery system, and timing are critical factors to consider.
- Because each person is different, what works for one person may be toxic for another. For best results, a customized program works best.
- Nutritional compounds administered in the form of a cocktail usually work best.
- There are three major groups of nutritional supplements, from the most gentle to the most potent:
    - Group 1: Gentle nutrients—vitamins, enzymes, and minerals
    - Group 2: glandulars and herbs
    - Group 3: Hormones, used as a last resort

Chapter 2

First Line of Defense — Gentle Nutrients

We use a group of first line nutrients we consider the most useful in helping the adrenals recover. Most with Adrenal Fatigue Syndrome, especially those with Adrenal Exhaustion, are internally over-stimulated due to an overactive sympathetic nervous system. That's why we believe in having the right non-stimulating natural supplements, those that help with recovery without further stimulating the already weak and tired adrenals.

Key members of this group possess common characteristics; in particular, they are intrinsically gentle and nurturing to the adrenal glands. It should be remembered, however, that no matter how intrinsically weak or gentle a compound is, the end result may differ significantly depending on the stage of adrenal weakness. It is not unusual for those with Stage 3D AFS to be intolerant to all supplements, even at extremely low doses. When individuals come to us for help, we teach them how to listen to the body's inner voice and correctly interpret the body's response to supplements.

Vitamin C: A Gentle Nutrient

Adrenal Fatigue Syndrome sufferers usually have an inadequate supply of many key nutrients. Out of these, subclinical vitamin C deficiency is the most prevalent. While no outward symptom of scurvy is seen, as happens in clinical vitamin C deficiency, the body;s need and appetite for vitamin C go up tremendously when the adrenals are weak.

Vitamin C is so gentle that most healthy people taking it would hardly notice any difference physically and mentally. This is, in fact, a hallmark of good health. Those with AFS, however, may have a different experience, depending on the level of weakness. Generally, the more advanced the adrenal weakness, the more vitamin C is needed. However, one can be more sensitive to vitamin C as well, due to a variety of reasons, thus it is not universally positive for everyone.

The adrenals contain one of the highest concentrations of vitamin C in the body, and this is where it is most needed, because it's a key catalyst of adrenal hormone production, including cortisol. Its antioxidant effects are particularly important in the presence of tissue-destroying oxidants in periodontal disease and other stealth infections that trigger AFS.

In addition to its critical adrenal support function, vitamin C is perhaps the best electron donor because of its water soluble properties and, thus, is readily bioavailable to the cells. Toxins deplete electron stores in the cell. Having sufficient electrons inside the body reverses potential cell death brought on by bacterial, environmental, and industrial toxins. In addition to its adrenal support function, vitamin C helps in the formation of critical collagens responsible for keeping the vascular and musculoskeletal systems pliable and healthy.

In times of stress, the body's requirement for vitamin C increases many fold. Having a sufficient level of vitamin C in the body is critical to help:

- make anti-inflammatory hormones, including cortisol
- prevent a catabolic state from worsening
- boost immune function to fight infection

- prevent heart disease
- overcome opportunistic infections, and
- neutralize systemic toxins from environmental and periodontal diseases

Proper vitamin C fortification should therefore be a cornerstone of any adrenal recovery program if tolerated.

Since humans are one of the few animals that cannot produce vitamin C, we are fortunate it is found abundantly in fruits and vegetables such as papayas, tomatoes, and Brussels sprouts, to name only three. However, relying on food sources alone for vitamin C is seldom sufficient in healing the adrenals, and much higher doses are needed. Remember, one orange delivers only about 65 mg of vitamin C. This is why nutritional supplements are recommended.

Most commercially available vitamin C is derived from corn sources. Those who are highly sensitive or allergic to corn can consider vitamin C derived from other food sources such as tapioca and acai berry instead.

Vitamin C is readily available, but it is also widely misused due to lack of knowledge. Choosing the proper combination of forms and delivery systems of vitamin C cocktails is an important clinical challenge for those with advanced adrenal weakness. It takes extensive clinical experience to create a personalized vitamin C cocktail that incorporates key attributes of each form and delivery system into a well designed, custom, nutritional cocktail to ensure sustained delivery without overstimulation.

Forms of Vitamin C

Vitamin C comes in many forms, each with its own properties and characteristics. Ascorbic acid, the most common form, is water soluble. It dissolves quickly in water and is excreted out of the body quickly, too. Because of its relative fast action, once absorbed, ascorbic acid tends to act quickly and therefore is described as "spiky." Effervescent forms of vitamin C are particularly prone to this characteristic. Those with a sensitive stomach or advanced AFS may find ascorbic acid hard to tolerate, especially in high doses.

Natural (from food) and synthetic ascorbic acid (from a tablet) are chemically identical. There appears to be no clinically significant difference in the bioavailability and bioactivity of natural and synthetic ascorbic acid.

The gastrointestinal absorption of ascorbic acid occurs through an active transport process, as well as through passive diffusion. At low gastrointestinal concentrations of ascorbic acid, active transport predominates, while at high gastrointestinal concentrations active transport becomes saturated, leaving only passive diffusion. This is where vitamin C is being absorbed without expanding energy from an area of high concentration to an area of low concentration passively. This form of transport is generally less efficient. As the amount of vitamin C intake increases, the overall absorption efficiency decreases. For example, a vitamin C intake of 180 mg is about 80-90 percent absorbed, but an intake of five grams is only 20 percent or less absorbed by most. Fortunately, this problem can be overcome with the liposomalized form of vitamin C discussed later and in Appendix C. Much of the excess vitamin C is removed from the body in the urine.

Mineral Ascorbates

These ascorbic acids are chemically bound or, in scientific terms, chelated to minerals as one unit. Commonly used minerals include calcium, sodium, and magnesium. These units, also called mineral salts of ascorbic acid, or commonly known as mineral ascorbates, are buffered and, therefore, less acidic. Thus, mineral ascorbates are often recommended to people who experience gastrointestinal problems (abdominal pain or diarrhea) with plain ascorbic acid. When taking large doses of mineral ascorbates, it is important to consider the dose of the mineral accompanying the ascorbic acid. Some minerals are more desirable than others.

Sodium ascorbate: 1,000 mg of sodium ascorbate contains 889 mg of ascorbic acid and 111 mg of sodium. Individuals following low-sodium diets (e.g., for high blood pressure) are generally advised to keep their total dietary sodium intake to less than 2,500 mg/day. However, most with advancing AFS develop low blood pressure due to inadequate sodium store. Administration of sodium ascorbate could significantly increase sodium intake and help blood pressure normalize. It is therefore the preferred form for Adrenal Fatigue Syndrome.

Calcium ascorbate: 1,000 mg of calcium ascorbate generally provides 890-910 mg of ascorbic acid and 90-110 mg of calcium. Calcium in this form appears to be reasonably well absorbed. Excessive calcium intake can sometimes worsen cardiac arrhythmia. Therefore, we don't recommend excessive intake. Ester-C® (a popular form of vitamin C) contains mainly calcium ascorbate, but also contains small amounts of the vitamin C metabolites: dehydroascorbic acid (oxidized ascorbic acid), calcium threonate, and trace levels of xylonate and lyxonate.

Potassium ascorbate: This form is not recommended for Adrenal Fatigue Syndrome in large amounts as most AFS sufferers already have high levels of potassium relative to sodium, though lab tests usually show both as normal.

Magnesium ascorbate: The recommended dietary allowance (RDA) for magnesium is 400-420 mg/day for adult men and 310-

320 mg/day for adult women. Magnesium helps to relieve tense muscles and acts as nature's powerful relaxant, making it a wonderful sleep aid.

Mineral Ascorbate Cocktail

For AFS, mineral ascorbates are best taken in a blend (such as Quantamax® discussed in Appendix G) including sodium, calcium, and magnesium ascorbates along with bioflavonoids and a small amount of ascorbic acid. They work well together. Not to be forgotten are important cofactors such as L-lysine, L-proline, malic acid, and citrus bioflavonoid. L-proline, L-lysine, and mineral ascorbates support collagen synthesis. Malic acid helps to increase energy, and along with magnesium, helps to stabilize gastric intestinal irritation and relax tense muscles. *Citrus* bioflavonoids help vitamin C to be made more bioavailable to the cell. *Potassium* ascorbates should be avoided in AFS.

Ascorbyl Palmitate

Ascorbyl palmitate is a fat soluble form of vitamin C. It is used as an antioxidant and preservative in foods, vitamins, drugs, and cosmetics. It is an amphipathic molecule. One end is water soluble and the other end is fat soluble. This dual solubility allows it to be incorporated into cell membranes. When incorporated into the membranes of human red blood cells, ascorbyl palmitate has been found to offer protection against oxidative damage and to protect vitamin E (a fat-soluble antioxidant) from destruction by free radicals.

Being fat soluble, it is absorbed into the cell membrane where ascorbic acid is unable to reach. Therefore, it is retained in the body for a longer period of time. Those with sensitivity to ascorbic acid will find this form particularly useful because of its gentleness.

Ascorbyl palmitate works best in a blend (such as C-Support detailed in Appendix G) with mineral ascorbates and citrus bioflavonoids as synergistic cofactors. Ascorbyl palmitate also acts synergistically with other antioxidants such as vitamin E.

Delivery Systems

The advance of nanotechnology and liposomal encapsulation technology offers a significantly enhanced oral liquid delivery system with superior absorption from the small intestine rather than from the stomach. The liposomal delivery system dramatically improves bioavailability and is by far the best oral form of vitamin C delivery if tolerated. A large amount of vitamin C can be delivered by liquid orally with a very high rate of absorption with this system, if used properly. Care should be taken to avoid any formula that contains alcohol as a preservative. (See Appendix C for a detailed discussion of this technology and ingredients to avoid.)

This system is ideally suited for Adrenal Fatigue Syndrome because high doses can be administered easily by mouth. Because absorption occurs at the small intestine and the stomach is bypassed, gastric irritation is minimal if any. Diarrhea is also significantly reduced because most is absorbed and does not remain in the GI tract where it triggers water retention at the large bowel. Nutritional cocktail blends (such as LipoNano® C detailed in Appendix G) rather than mono-therapy works best. Important synergistic co-factors that enhance effectiveness include alpha lipoic acid, and grape seed extract / polygonum cuspidatum.

While the bioavailability of vitamin C delivered by liposome is far superior to other forms of vitamin C, ascorbic acid in its various forms still has its place and should not be ignored. The absorption tends to be faster and the results more immediate. Because each body reacts differently to vitamin C, no one-size-fits-all protocol exists. A thorough knowledge of these forms is important. Various forms of ascorbates, including regular and liposomal vitamin C, should be used together in a nutritional blend or cocktail mix for maximum and sustained effect. Taking the right combination can go a long ways toward AFS recovery. Well formulated vitamin C blends tend to be more expensive compared to plain ascorbic acid, but well worth the cost, especially for those with advancing AFS.

Vitamin C Safety

Over the years, many research studies have concluded that vitamin C is one of the safest and most nontoxic natural nutrients we can take. Both long term and high oral intake of up to 20,000 mg and intravenous doses of up to 300,000 mg of vitamin C are safe and have no side effects. Likewise, studies show no evidence of toxicity or side effects when late-stage cancer patients are given up to 50,000 mg of intravenous vitamin C daily for up to eight weeks. Moreover, AIDS patients were given anywhere between 25,000 to 125,000 mg of vitamin C on a regular basis based on bowel tolerance without any side effects. Vitamin C is undeniably a safe supplement even when given in high doses over a long period of time in healthy adults.

We have seen reports of heartburn in some people (primarily in those with a sensitive gastric lining) while using vitamin C. Diarrhea is also a common occurrence when the intake of vitamin C exceeds the body's bowl tolerance level (BTL). This is a temporary effect and subsides once vitamin C dosage is reduced. This is not considered a side effect but rather a sign of maximum saturation from oral ingestion.

Those with Adrenal Fatigue Syndrome, especially in the advanced stage, may experience increased anxiety and or fatigue when taking vitamin C. This is generally due to a clearance problem related to the liver and not the vitamin itself. Vitamin C is broken down into metabolites prior to its excretion from the body. If this breakdown process is dysfunctional or functions sub-optimally (as we frequently see in advanced adrenal weakness), the speed of clearance is reduced. As a result, metabolites accumulate and circulate in the body for a longer period of time. These excessive circulating metabolites can trigger a wide variety of re-toxification reactions, with symptoms including malaise, joint pain, anxiety, fatigue, heart palpitations, and so forth, which are not side effects of vitamin C. We usually see these symptoms reverse by themselves as liver function improves.

Vitamin C and Iron

Vitamin C enhances iron absorption many fold, but it must be taken simultaneously with the iron so both vitamin C and iron are present together in the intestine. If additional iron absorption is not desired, then vitamin C and iron can be taken two hours apart.

Note: Those with *hemochromatosis*, a disorder in which high amounts of iron build up in the body, should take only moderate levels of vitamin C.

Vitamin C and Kidney Stones

Since studies have shown that vitamin C contributes to the increased production of oxalates in the body, it is commonly linked with a buildup of kidney stones. However, no evidence has surfaced to pinpoint vitamin C as the sole culprit in the increase in kidney stones, and other factors exist that contribute to oxalate development.

When ingested, vitamin C is broken down into dehydroascorbic acid (DHAA) and further metabolized and converted into diketogulonic acid. Finally, it is broken down and metabolized into lyxonic, xylose, threonic acid, or oxalic acid (oxalate). Oxalate is the metabolic end product after the human body breaks down vitamin C. The body cannot break oxalates down into smaller compounds. Confusion arises because of the presence of calcium oxalate, the primary component of kidney stones. Moreover, some suggest that the intake of vitamin C promotes the development of these kidney stones due to the oxalates produced when vitamin C is broken down by the human body. However, studies have shown that these theories are not well supported.

A number of factors cause a buildup of calcium oxalate stones in the kidney. High vitamin C intake when certain medical conditions are present is just one of many. Kidney stones are linked to the presence of heavy metal chelating agents such as DMPS and EDTA. Taking vitamin C may increase the oxalate level in the urine, which is why many believe prolonged use of the vitamin increases calcium oxalates in the body. However, other research shows a leveling of oxalate production even though vitamin C dosing was continued. Furthermore, the human body excretes significant amounts of oral vitamin C without being metabolized. In addition, in order for the body to use vitamin C, it doesn't need to be broken down to oxalates. As much as 89 percent of vitamin C administered is eliminated as DHAA.

Dietary sources of oxalates include: spinach, rhubarb, parsley, citrus fruits, and especially tea. Likewise, Swiss chard, cocoa, chocolate, pepper, wheat germ, peanuts, refried beans, lime peel, and various soy-based foods also have high oxalate content. High protein foods such as sardines and herring roe also increase oxalate secretion in the body.

Those who take excessive calcium supplements, especially the elderly, may need to be more careful. Excess calcium from supplements finds its way to other compounds in the body. For example, the calcium combines with oxalates already present in high concentrations. However, studies show that vitamin C taken with calcium carbonate and other oxalate sources can facilitate stone formation. Therefore, individuals who have kidney stones should take sodium ascorbate as a vitamin C supplement and should reduce calcium ascorbate as well as regular calcium supplements.

For patients with kidney problems, it's necessary to monitor vitamin C therapy as well as other oxalate sources as a safety precaution. Totally avoiding vitamin C is not a sound recommendation since the human body still needs this vitamin, whether AFS is present or not. In normal individuals, no conclusive evidence has pinpointed vitamin C as the sole cause of renal and kidney failure caused by excess calcium oxalate crystal formation. In some people, the decline in kidney function after vitamin C therapy is more likely related to dehydration and pre-existing kidney disease. In fact, these are two major causes of the decline in kidney function, not vitamin C therapy. Before blaming vitamin C for decline in kidney function, we need to study the person's medical history. When using any medication or nutrient, proper hydration is always necessary and helps prevent crystallization as well as concentration of precipitates (solid substances made from liquids) in the human body, which includes kidney stone crystals.

Vitamin C and G6PD Deficiency

Likewise, the same caution about vitamin C is necessary for those with G6PD deficiency (glucose-6-phosphate dehydrogenase deficiency, a genetic disorder affecting red blood cells).

Iron levels in G6PD deficient cells detrimentally interact with vitamin C, and G6PD deficient cells rupture due to the presence of vitamin C. Vitamin C, in rare cases, can promote a hemolytic (related to red blood cells) crisis in individuals with G6PD, although this is difficult to predict. If using vitamin C, this group of patients should be supervised.

Vitamin C and Thyroid Medication

Some with hypothyroidism take thyroid medication but aren't able to achieve their target serum TSH level. However, research has found that vitamin C, along with levothyroxine (a thyroid hormone), decreases TSH levels substantially, by as much as 27 percent. Studies have shown that over a period of six weeks, taking levothyroxine along with 1 gram of vitamin C mixed with water was able to help the majority of patients achieve their TSH target level. Taking vitamin C along with levothyroxine medications should be considered in patients with difficulties in the absorption of levothyroxine. Those recovering from Adrenal Fatigue Syndrome with vitamin C support are likely to find their need for thyroid medication reduces as their recovery continues.

Vitamin C Tolerance and Withdrawal

As you take more vitamin C, your body adapts and gets used to higher levels. This tolerance is normal, but if you reduce vitamin C intake, do so gradually. A 300-500 mg reduction every week is usually safe. A sudden drop in vitamin C intake can trigger symptoms of scurvy, such as bleeding gums and easy bruising. If you experience these symptoms as you reduce vitamin C intake, slow down the rate of reduction. If your fatigue returns and worsens, it may be a sign that your body needs more vitamin C. Always consult your healthcare professional for guidance if you have such experiences. The body will adapt to the lower dosage over time, though the adaptation to lower doses is usually slower than adaptation to higher doses.

Dosage Consideration: **The current RDA for vitamin C is 75 mg for women and 90 mg for men. We believe that those with AFS require much more.**

- **Commercially available oral liposomal vitamin C, such as LipoNano® C, is the preferred delivery system. The dosage varies greatly from person to person, but most do well with 200 to 3,000 mg a day. Because this is a high potency form, always start at very low doses to ensure tolerance.**
- **Mineral ascorbates (preferably a proper blend of sodium, calcium, and magnesium ascorbate) dosage ranges from 200 to 2,000 mg a day.**
- **For fat soluble vitamin C with bioflavonoid, the dosages range from 200-1000 mg a day.**
- **Avoid effervescent and chewable forms of vitamin C.**

Those whose fatigue becomes significantly worse, or experience increased anxiety upon intake of vitamin C, should stop and seek professional advice. These paradoxical reactions are more prevalent as AFS advances.

As we've said, we see significant individual differences in the way the body accepts the various forms of vitamin C, which makes it critical that those with moderate and severe Adrenal Fatigue Syndrome consult a healthcare professional rather than embarking on a self-navigation program. Only those with very mild Adrenal Fatigue should self-navigate. The more advanced the AFS, the more critical it is to properly adjust the dosage to fit the body's weakened state. Otherwise, we risk worsening AFS.

Vitamin C is a wonderful natural tool. Most therapeutic failures arise from improper use or lack of knowledge about how to deliver this important nutrient in a cocktail to the cells through various forms and delivery systems.

Glutathione (GSH)

Excessive oxidative stress is implicated in premature aging, chronic degenerative disease, cancer, and diseases such as Alzheimer's. As you breathe, your body constantly reacts with oxygen as your cells generate energy, and consequently, produce free radicals, which are highly reactive molecules. These free radicals interact with other molecules in the cells, resulting in what we call oxidative stress that damages proteins and other cell components.

Oxidative stress also contributes to a host of *subclinical* dysfunctions, such as chronic fatigue, fibromyalgia, and Adrenal Fatigue Syndrome. The body has natural antioxidants available to neutralize undesirable effects of oxidative stress, one of which is glutathione.

When a person experiences an increase in oxidative stress, the levels of glutathione in the cells drop, which is a precursor to the death of cells. Unhealthy cells are compromised in their abilities to produce adequate amounts of glutathione to protect the body against harmful external toxins or free radicals. These cellular level battles within the body go on without our knowledge, of course, and can have catastrophic effects if the process is hampered in any way.

Glutathione detoxifies harmful chemicals such as lead, mercury, xenobiotics (a chemical present, but not normally produced or expected to be found in an organism), toxic metabolites, and pesticides that have accumulated in the cell. Maintaining sufficient intracellular glutathione levels is one of the key and most powerful lines of defense against cellular death. Glutathione is also considered a powerful detoxifier in the body.

Glutathione supports and protects the immune system and neutralizes oxidative damage caused by toxins and pathogens. Aside from these protective functions, glutathione also maintains the transport of amino acids. It also sustains the synthesis of DNA, protein, and prostaglandin (a family of hormones). These functions rely on glutathione to fight against degenerative diseases, cancer, infections, and in Adrenal Fatigue Syndrome, a situation in which the body is rapidly decompensating.

Electron Flow

Glutathione promotes the healthy flow of electrons and maintains their steady supply in the body's cells. This is the source of its effectiveness. Simply put, hindering the flow of electrons or robbing the cells of electrons is detrimental for health. The opposite also is true. When electron flow is abundant and smooth, cells are healthy and live longer. Poor flow of electrons corresponds to low energy, higher disease rates, low cell integrity, and cell death.

Glutathione donates electrons to the body's antioxidant pool, including antioxidants such as vitamin C, vitamin E, alpha-lipoic acid, and superoxide dismutase (SOD). In addition, glutathione neutralizes disease-causing oxidants and is capable of eliminating heavy metals. By protecting the body from free radicals and pathogenic attacks, it is keeping the cellular structure intact.

The Master Recycler

Glutathione is the most powerful antioxidant at the intracellular level and works synergistically with vitamin C, a key antioxidant in the extracellular level. Glutathione also recharges nutrients such as carnitine, vitamin E, and alpha-lipoic acid. After performing its antioxidant function, vitamin C is recycled and is accompanied by glutathione. This makes glutathione a part of the recycling chain in the body that allows it to reuse natural compounds without decreasing the benefits derived by the body. Glutathione is called the *master recycler*, and as such it keeps vitamin C in an electron donating state and plays a role in recharging vitamin C. To reciprocate, vitamin C alleviates the effect of glutathione deficiency and cellular death. In other words, vitamin C and glutathione mutually support and enhance the functions of each other.

Almost all diseases and toxins cause death and sickness by stealing electrons at the cellular level. This is why we know depleted electrons are part of chronic disease. Conditions such as Adrenal Fatigue Syndrome are part of a spectrum of low energy states where the body's energy output is reduced. The body's electrons are the fuel of life and are responsible for generating energy necessary to sustain life. To achieve optimum health and reverse this low energy state, a good flow of electrons is necessary. To achieve this, principal antioxidants, including glutathione, vitamin C, and vitamin E, work synergistically to replenish cells depleted of electrons. By helping each other supply and recycle electrons to the cells, the body can recover at the cellular level.

Dosage Consideration: Glutathione is a free amino acid peptide (substances derived from combinations of amino acids). The regular form of glutathione breaks down in the stomach before entering the blood stream. For best results, consider oral liposomal forms such as LipoNano® Glutathione (detailed in Appendix G).

Oral liposomal technology dramatically improves the bioavailability of glutathione. Bypassing the stomach, such liposomal encapsulated glutathione is absorbed in the small intestine and transported to the circulatory system directly. Consider 100-800 mg per day via liposomal encapsulation technology, such as LipoNano® Glutathione.

Pantethine/Pantothenic Acid

Few natural compounds are more powerful than pantethine and its relative, pantothenic acid. For decades, we've known that pantothenic acid is one of the essential nutrients we can use to help adrenal function. In fact, it is a good substitute for prednisone, a drug with serious and awful side effects, although it effectively treats autoimmune diseases including arthritis, allergies, and colitis.

Once inside the body, pantothenic acid forms a substance called pantethine, which is further converted into an enzyme called *co-enzyme A*. An extremely important compound, co-enzyme A is essential in the metabolism of protein, fat, and carbohydrates. It is also the starting point for the body's production of adrenal steroids, cholesterol, bile, and hemoglobin.

While pantothenic acid ultimately leads to coenzyme A, using pantethine is a much faster way to achieve the same effect as pantothenic acid and with intense potency. Pantethine allows the adrenal glands to generate more of the anti-stress hormone, cortisol, thereby reducing the body's inflammatory response. For maximum effect, it should be used in conjunction with a nutritional cocktail of vitamin C; bioflavonoids (substances found in plants and plant pigments that act as antioxidants); other antioxidants such as pine bark extract, ascorbyl palmitate (a fat soluble form of a type of vitamin C); and cofactors such as lysine, proline, glutamine, glycine, and carnitine (a derivative of lysine).

Pantethine helps reduce blood levels of triglycerides and promotes healthy cholesterol levels as well. A daily dose of 900 mg has been shown to reduce triglycerides by up to 32 percent, along with a 19 percent drop in total cholesterol and a 21 percent drop in LDL cholesterol (low density lipoprotein, the type of cholesterol considered bad). At the same time, HDL cholesterol (the good cholesterol) rose by 23 percent. Pantethine also protects the heart and arteries and acts synergistically with vitamin E against cholesterol build up.

Pantethine also helps increase the production of omega-3 fatty acids in the body (EPA, DHA, and other essential fats). Omega-3 fatty acids have powerful anti-inflammatory effects and reduce the clot promoting fats in cell membranes. Most spectacularly, pantethine produces no side effects.

Pantethine is furthermore an excellent nutrient to use with two major gastrointestinal problems, colitis, and Crohn's disease. A daily dose of 900-1200 mg of pantethine matched with 900-1200 mg of pantothenic acid drastically improves the two conditions. Improvement usually kicks in four to eight weeks after starting this combination, but many have reported benefits in much shorter time. Pantethine also helps promote the growth of beneficial intestinal bacteria. Further, it helps the body combat the overgrowth of yeast in the body and the accumulation of other toxic substances such as formaldehyde. Therefore, pantethine is a gentle, natural detoxifier.

Pantothenic acid, while not as strong as pantethine, has its own role. For example, in high doses (up to 10 grams a day), it can help with acne. Some people have reported reduced inflammation and improved symptoms of burning foot syndrome. It is also used in conjunction with non-steroidal anti-inflammatory drugs for arthritis.

Overall, pantethine is a remarkably safe and extremely valuable natural dietary supplement that is used for Adrenal Fatigue Syndrome, along with supporting normal cholesterol and triglyceride levels.

Dosage Consideration: **Consider 300-1200 mg a day of pantethine along with pantothenic acid in a blend, such as Pandrenal® (discussed in Appendix G). Combination therapy offers the best clinical efficacy as both components are needed and they work well together unless a person is very sensitive. Much higher doses may be needed in AFS with the supervision of a healthcare professional.**

Phosphatidylcholine (Lecithin)

Phosphatidylcholine (PC) is an excellent cell protector, especially for those in our nervous system. Soybeans and eggs are good sources. PC also serves as the main source of choline, which in turn is essential to form acetylcholine, an important neurotransmitter of the ANS mentioned earlier in Chapter 8, *Stage 3B—Hormonal Axis Imbalances.* Choline, on the other hand, is essential for our bodies to manufacture our own lecithin. When you buy lecithin from the health food store, you are buying a natural concentrate containing PC plus a mixture of other similar compounds, called phospholipids.

PC is a key nutrient in the health of the nerve, as it protects the inner cell from external insult. It is therefore good for a variety of nerve disorders, including tingling, memory impairment, Alzheimer's disease, and strokes. Remember that those with advanced AFS are invariably afflicted with some form of ANS, autonomic nervous system, dysregulation. Having the proper amount of PC in the body helps cushion that dysfunction. It also fights heart disease and enhances liver function to process fats. It has been shown to retard fatty liver progression. PC is also an important component of female hormone balancing. It helps the liver to convert estradiol, the form of estrogen with great cancer causing potential, into estriol, a safer, less potent, but less carcinogenic form of the hormone. Estrogen dominance, as we have already seen, is a major problem in those with advanced AFS, and PC can help.

Dosage Consideration: **Lecithin granules are easily available and can be used in everyday meal preparation. They are great additions to recipes and a great salad garnish. PC supplementation in pill form is most convenient for most. Bear in mind that these contain usually only about 50 percent of PC by weight. Up to 35 grams per day has been used safely and well tolerated. Additional vitamin C should be included because vitamin C serves to protect us from the nitrosamines (a group of potentially harmful chemicals), which can be generated as choline is metabolized.**

NADH

NAD (nicotinamide adenine dinucleotide) plays an important role in the energy production pathway of our body. The reduced form (with a hydrogen added) of NAD, called NADH or coenzyme 1, is the specific way by which all our cells get their energy. The body normally makes its own NADH from niacinamide (a form of niacin, vitamin B3), but aging and chronic diseases slow this conversion.

> **NADH is the quintessential energy giving compound, but not everyone can tolerate it. In the brain, NADH helps neurons make dopamine, a catecholamine neurotransmitter. Recall that dopamine is the chemical precursor of norepinephrine and epinephrine. Too much dopamine can therefore enhance catecholamine flow. This can worsen those who already have reactive sympathoadrenal response, as in Stage 3C Adrenal Exhaustion. Those who are constitutionally weak or sensitive may find this nutrient too spiky, with the potential of worsening anxiety and insomnia. In extreme cases, adrenal crashes may be precipitated. Fortunately, this is usually due to inappropriate dosage, usually a dosage that's too high.**
> ***Dosage Consideration:* 2.5-20 mg as tolerated.**

Vitamin E

Vitamin E is a great antioxidant. Free radicals generated internally by the adrenal glands during hormone synthesis need to be neutralized. Vitamin E performs this function inside the adrenal glands and throughout the body. It also helps to recycle vitamin C. High amounts of vitamin E are therefore needed for the adrenals to maintain optimal steroid production. This is particularly important during the recovery process. Because vitamin E is fat soluble, excessive amounts are not indicated. In addition, because it is metabolized through the liver, those with the low clearance issue we see so often in advanced Adrenal Exhaustion should use caution.

Vitamin E comes in many forms. The d-alpha-tocopherol form is natural and the preferred form, though a cocktail of mixed tocopherols is best for AFS. Because vitamin E is not a direct ingredient in hormone synthesis within the adrenal glands, its actions are slow. Allow three months of consistent intake to enjoy the benefit.

***Dosage Consideration:* 400-800 IU of mixed tocopherol daily. Because vitamin E has blood thinning properties, those on blood thinning medications need to be monitored.**

Inosital

While this compound does not directly support adrenal function, it is an excellent natural relative of the B-complex family. It relieves nervous tension and encourages sounder sleep. Specifically, inosital levels are often lower than average in people hospitalized for depression. Resupplying inosital can lift spirits. Those with anxiety and obsessive-compulsive disorders (OCDs) also benefit, though higher doses may be required.

Fresh produce, whole grains, and red meats are good sources of inosital, and these food sources could supply up to 1 gram a day. However, a large amount could be in the form of fiber, thus not well absorbed. For this reason we recommend supplements.

Dosage Consideration: **For everyday uses such as temporary anxiety and insomnia, 500-2000 mg at bedtime. Clinical depression and OCDs require much higher doses, up to 18 grams, as shown in research studies. Because inosital is a chemical relative of glucose, those with sugar imbalances and carbohydrate intolerance may experience intolerance and must be careful.**

D-ribose

Ribose is a sugar molecule made from the body's glucose and is a vital component of ATP (adenosine triphosphate). Scientists consider ATP to be the energy currency, in that it is a high energy molecule that stores the energy we need. We can also think of it as a rechargeable battery. Ribose, an essential of ATP, rapidly restores energy, especially in diseased hearts and other muscles that need energy. Until the 1940s, D-ribose was believed to be a structural component of DNA and RNA, but with very little physiological importance. However, subsequent studies in the 1950s concluded that D-ribose actually plays a significant role in the metabolic reaction known as *pentose phosphate pathway.* This pathway is pivotal in many functions, including synthesizing energy and producing genetic material (the components of a cell that determine its structure and the ability to regenerate). It also provides substances used by certain tissues that produce fatty acids and hormones.

We have a great deal of human and animal research showing positive results from D-ribose in terms of improving energy and the function of the heart and other muscles. In addition, using D-ribose does not negatively affect the action of common drugs used in the treatment of heart disease.

When D-ribose is used with two other nutrients, L-carnitine and CoQ10, and integrated into AFS protocol, energy delivery is nearly always helped. This is also a useful nutritional cocktail to support heart health and many more conditions related to cardiovascular disease.

D-ribose is not a well known nutrient, but in the right setting, it is an excellent nutrient to enhance energy output. For this reason, this nutrient is important in dealing with conditions such as chronic fatigue, Adrenal Fatigue Syndrome, and cardiac weakness.

Anyone wishing more energy, gently delivered, can consider D-ribose. Unlike other nutrients, we don't refer to deficiencies of D-ribose in the tissues, that is, a lower amount or quantity than what is normal. The liver, adrenal glands, and fat tissues produce the most D-ribose, while others produce very little. Tissues relying most on aerobic energy metabolism, meaning they are reliant on oxygen, such as the heart and muscles, are affected by ATP drain, meaning they are severely affected by any amount of energy deprivation. D-ribose supplementation is the solution to this, because it gives back the energy. This is one reason for the success of D-ribose in cardiac patients.

We use D-ribose to help increase energy reserves during adrenal crashes, restore energy stores before and after exercise in those with AFS, and for those whom we believe will benefit from replenishing energy.

In essence, D-ribose, a naturally occurring sugar in the body, is regularly produced by our various tissues. Taking D-ribose supplements gives your body a little bit more of it to prevent fatigue and weak functioning. However, it is important to remember that D-ribose supplement studies have limitations. For example, studies have not included a placebo group or included long term follow up.

D-ribose supplements are easily absorbed by the body—about 97 percent is absorbed. Some individuals need a high dosage, i.e. those with low energy states, such as we see in advanced Adrenal Fatigue Syndrome, fibromyalgia, and chronic fatigue, and others who have difficulty delivering oxygen to their tissues. Those with sugar imbalances or carbohydrate intolerance may experience adrenal crashes with this compound. Therefore, for best results, we use D-ribose only under appropriate clinical conditions, and we don't recommend self-navigating.

If your health provider recommends D-ribose, always eat some food when you take it. Even a handful of nuts will suffice, but do not take this on an empty stomach. Because it is a form of sugar, those who are prone to blood sugar imbalances or have insulin or sugar sensitivity may develop reactive hypoglycemia if the body is not used to this nutrient. At high doses, side effects can include lightheadedness and mild diarrhea.

Note: Although no known contraindications of D-ribose therapy exist, we recommend that pregnant women, nursing mothers, and young children do not take it. We also recommend that you ask your doctor to advise you before taking D-ribose supplements.

Dosage Consideration: 1-10 grams daily to prevent cardiovascular disease, for adrenal support, for athletes on maintenance, and for others engaged in strenuous activity.

D-ribose is available in various forms. The powder form is the most common and bioavailable. We recommend including cofactors such as L-carnitine, co-enzyme

Q10, and alpha-lipoic acid in a supplement regimen because they also enhance energy production and work synergistically with D-ribose.

Collagen

Collagen is the most abundant protein in the human body. It is critical in maintaining the health of the connective tissues that line the blood vessels, and it also contributes to the supporting framework upon which skeletal muscles operate. It reduces the catabolic (breakdown) state typically experienced by advanced Adrenal Fatigue Syndrome sufferers with symptoms of muscle wasting. As is obvious, for optimum health, we need proper collagen synthesis.

Collagen production occurs in several stages, and the three key components are vitamin C, and the amino acids lysine and proline. Over twenty types of collagen exist, but Type I collagen is the most abundant in the human body. It is present in the skin, scar tissue, artery walls, tendons, and the organic parts of bones and teeth. Type III collagen is the second most abundant collagen in human tissues and occurs particularly in tissues exhibiting elastic properties. It is the collagen of granulation tissue (fibrous connective tissue) and is produced quickly by young fibroblasts, which are involved in synthesizing collagen, before the tougher Type I collagen is synthesized.

Around age thirty-five, collagen Types I and III decline, which is when skin loses its elasticity and wrinkles form.

In advanced Adrenal Fatigue Syndrome, the body breaks down collagen and muscle for fuel, a process that weakens the skeletal system. This is why we see symptoms such as fibromyalgia, chronic muscular pain of unknown origin, joint pain, loss of muscle tone, and reduced muscle strength. In order for the body to heal, this collagen must be replaced with the main building blocks of collagen: glycine, proline, lysine, and vitamin C. Of these, the body can manufacture only proline (from the amino acid glutamine).

Fortunately, collagen is readily available as a nutritional supplement and can be taken orally. Types I and III collagen are particularly well suited for Adrenal Fatigue Syndrome. This strategy is particularly useful before and after exercise. Hydrolyzed powdered form of these two types are available and promote maximum absorption within the body. It is important to use 100 percent pure collagen.

Dosage Consideration: **3-15 grams of Type I and III blended as needed.**

Note: Excessive intake may lead to constipation and gastric discomfort especially in those with advanced Adrenal Exhaustion.

Probiotics

A healthy intestinal track is of paramount importance because gastrointestinal function is invariably compromised in advancing AFS. Common GI symptoms include constipation, poor food assimilation, bloating, and irritable bowel. Optimal gastrointestinal health depends on the balance of microscopic interplay between billions of beneficial (good) and pathogenic (bad) bacteria; the body needs both for normal bowel functions.

About 400 species of these "good bugs" inhabit the intestines and their total population is about 100 times the number of cells in your body. Remarkably, these microorganisms coexist peacefully in a carefully balanced internal ecosystem. As long as they flourish, they prevent the pathogenic, disease causing bacteria and fungi from colonizing. In this way, beneficial bacteria help keep you healthy. If the delicate intestinal environment is disrupted, pathogenic bacteria, parasites, and fungi such as clostridia, salmonella, staphylococcus, *blastocystis hominis,* and *Candida albicans* often move in, multiply, and then attack the beneficial bacteria.

Considerable research shows us that good bacteria, otherwise known as *probiotics*, help defend our bodies from the disease causing species of bacteria and also detoxify toxic chemicals. Beneficial bacteria also produce valuable vitamins including biotin, folic acid, niacin, pantothenic acid, riboflavin, thiamin, vitamin B6, vitamin B12, and vitamin K. These bacteria also assist in breaking down dietary proteins into amino acids, which are then reconfigured into new proteins useful for the body. Good bacteria also ensure that toxins are excreted from the bowels (via the stool) rather than being absorbed into the bloodstream.

Acidophilus is an example of a beneficial probiotic in that they stimulate activity in the thymus and spleen (key immune system glands). They prompt the body to manufacture natural antibodies. Certain acidophilus strains even protect against the formation of tumors and promote production of interferon, a hormone that protects against cancer. When probiotics are present, they secrete mediators in which the pathogenic forms cannot grow. However, in the absence of probiotics, the pathogenic micro-organic forms take over and their toxins exclude the probiotics. This is one reason replacing our natural flora and keeping our bowels healthy and populated with probiotics is vital in preventing disease. Probiotics containing Lactobacillus acidophilus and Bifida can help detoxification programs.

Numerous studies help us understand the way probiotics work and establish the many beneficial and therapeutic aspects of probiotics. These include:

- Increased enzyme production, such as proteases, which digest proteins and lipases that digest fats.
- Improved bowel transit time and texture of the stool.
- Increased synthesis of immune antibodies and augmentation of gamma-interferon production.
- Reduction of lactose intolerance caused by a deficiency of the enzyme lactase, which leads to reduced bloating, gas formation, and stomach discomfort after milk consumption.
- Acts as an antitoxin with anti-carcinogenic and antitumor agents.
- Relief of dermatitis and other skin disorders by improving the balance of gastrointestinal bacteria.

Many scientists at the forefront of probiotics research believe that the toxins secreted from the pathogens, rather than the pathogens, are responsible for diseases. Probiotics help reduce the amount of toxic chemicals in the body, namely pathogenic bacteria and fungi, which produce their own toxins. At a local level, this minimizes the risk of colon cancers, protects the entire body, and improves overall health on a larger scale.

We can repopulate the beneficial bacteria by regularly supplementing with probiotics such as acidophilus. These microorganisms restore and maintain balance within your internal ecosystem while displacing noxious bacteria and fungi at the same time. They also increase the acidity of the intestinal environment that probiotics thrive in and harmful bugs detest. (As an aside, acidophilus literally means "love of acid.")

Acidophilus supplements are widely available in health food stores and drugstores, although it can be a daunting task to select among the numerous "something-dophilus" products. However, if you examine the labels you will discover a variety of useful bugs including *Lactobacillus acidophilus, Bifidobacterium bifidum, Lactobacillus bulgaricus,* and *Streptococcus faecium.* Some products may contain fructooligosaccharides, which are sugars that nourish beneficial bacteria to make them colonize faster. All of these ingredients are acceptable and any combination of them works well.

Acidophilus supplements contain living organisms, so freshness is critical. Purchase a product well before its expiration date, which should be clearly displayed. Once the supplements are opened, keep them refrigerated.

Dosage Consideration: 1-4 tablets before meals. **Potency varies greatly from one product to another. It is best to refer to the instructions on the product label. For those who don't want to use these supplements, certain yogurt products contains the friendly bacterium *Lactobacillus acidophilus*, which can help restore intestinal micro-flora balance and inhibit the growth of potentially harmful bacteria.**

Digestive Enzymes

Found in abundance in the body (over 1300 types), enzymes are molecule catalysts; they are considered the construction workers that facilitate all the bodily functions. For example, raw fruits and vegetables contain a plentiful supply of enzymes, *but cooking and food processing can destroy them.* When enzymes are destroyed, this affects the body's ability to digest food, deliver nutrients, and optimally perform its functions. Thus, toxins build up and accumulate in the body.

Digestive enzymes are especially important, as poor food assimilation is one of the main symptoms of AFS. Because plant enzymes help digest our food directly through the intestinal tract, supplemental enzymes help prevent feelings of bloating and exhaustion after a big meal. We consume an average of two pounds of food per day or twenty tons over a lifetime. Smooth passage of food through the gastrointestinal tract is critical to avoid stasis of feces, which releases toxins. Together with a diet high in soluble fiber, digestive enzymes help digestion.

Digestive enzymes also help other vitamins and minerals. For example, the fat soluble vitamins A, D, E, and K require fat for absorption. Fat must be broken down by an enzyme known as lipase. If lipase is not present in sufficient quantities, the fat will not be broken down, and if that happens, the vitamins are not released. Therefore, you can spend a fortune on vitamin pills, *but in the absence of the proper enzymes to release the vitamins into the body, the body flushes the vitamins out rather than using them.*

If our organs start to degenerate and fail to function properly, the stress of this process most likely shows up on the face. However, after consuming digestive enzymes one of the early signs of better digestion is improvement in skin tone. Digestive enzymes can therefore play a key role in adrenal support among those with dysregulated gastric assimilation.

> ***Dosage Consideration: 1-4 enzyme tablets before meal as tolerated.*** **Potency varies greatly from one product to another. It is best to refer to the instructions on the product label.**

Phosphatidylserine

Phosphatidylserine is a major component of nerve cell production and is sometimes used to enhance memory. It also reduces cortisol levels, as shown in research studies of otherwise healthy men engaging in vigorous exercise. Vigorous exercise is expected to increase cortisol but in the subjects phosphaditylserine was found to reduce post-exercise cortisol. In addition, testosterone levels, normally expected to drop after intense exercise, were not reduced and their perceived level of well-being immediately following exercise was positive.

These experiments are important because they show that phosphaditylserine is able to reduce cortisol levels when the body experiences stress. These studies used exercise to produce the stress, but the same principle holds for other types of mental or physical stress. This makes phosphaditylserine a valuable tool for controlling cortisol levels.

Bear in mind, however, that not all exercise results in increased cortisol production. For example, short term, moderate exercise does not increase cortisol concentration in plasma at all, and only minor changes in cortisol concentration occur during more intensive exercise lasting less than one hour. In practical terms, this means we don't need to avoid exercise for fear of boosting our cortisol level, and a game of tennis, a bike ride, or a walk around the block will not increase cortisol production. In fact, the stress reducing benefits of moderate exercise help keep cortisol in check. Physical activity also promotes cardiovascular health and mental acuity, helping us maintain a higher quality of life as we age.

> ***Dosage Consideration:* 200-1000 mg. Those with high nighttime cortisol and sleep onset insomnia may find this particularly helpful. Beware of paradoxical reactions in those with advanced Adrenal Fatigue Syndrome for reasons not known.**

Vitamin B12

Vitamin B12 helps maintain red blood cells and nerve cells as well as protecting against a variety of conditions. Vitamin B12 also boosts energy. It is also needed to make DNA. It reduces homocysteine, an amino acid now known to promote atherosclerosis. Vitamin B12 deficiency produces symptoms similar to Alzheimer's disease.

B12 is found in animal foods such as meat, poultry, and dairy products, most of which should be consumed in moderation by those with AFS. Those over age fifty might have decreased stomach acid, which makes it difficult to separate the B12 which is bound to protein. In addition, vegans, the type of vegetarian who does not consume dairy products or eggs, are especially vulnerable to B12 deficiency and should take supplements.

***Dosage Consideration:* 100-1000 mcg. Many forms are available. The sublingual form is the fastest acting. Those who are sensitive or weak need to be extra careful because of the potential for overstimulation. If you decide to stop taking vitamin B12 supplementation, do not do so abruptly.**

Magnesium

Magnesium (Mg) is an ubiquitous element in nature. Both plants and animals have an absolute requirement for magnesium, a mineral that plays a central role in photosynthesis in plants and many of the metabolic reactions in animals. Magnesium is a cofactor in over 300 enzymatic reactions in human beings. It is required for sodium, potassium, and calcium homeostasis, as well as for the formation, transfer, storage, and utilization of ATP (mentioned earlier as the energy currency in the body) at the cellular level. You cannot live without magnesium. The lower the cellular level of magnesium, the faster energy flow is depleted. It's that simple. Therefore, we can't underestimate its importance in optimizing adrenal function.

Magnesium works synergistically with vitamin C and pantothenic acid in steroid synthesis. As important as magnesium is, only about 25 percent of Americans meet the Recommended Dietary Allowance (RDA) of 300-400 mg per day for magnesium. Most American women get only 175-225 mg per day; men get 220-260 mg. Current statistics show that only 25 percent of surveyed populations have a magnesium intake *at or greater* than the RDA. In addition, almost 40 percent consume less than 70 percent of the RDA. It is fair to say that the majority of the North American population has a suboptimal intake of magnesium.

To get enough magnesium from diet, one needs to consume about 2000 calories a day. Nuts, whole grains, and legumes are high in magnesium. There is a poor correlation between blood magnesium and intracellular levels. Total body magnesium levels may decrease 20 percent during a fast, with no change in blood levels. While low blood magnesium levels may correctly indicate serious disease, a "normal" magnesium blood level by traditional laboratory testing may exist concurrently with a deficit in intracellular magnesium.

Common symptoms of magnesium deficiency include:

- Musculoskeletal symptoms: osteoporosis, chronic fatigue and weakness, muscle spasms, tics, tremors, and restlessness.
- Cardiovascular symptoms: atherosclerosis, cardiac arrhythmias, sudden death, and vasospasms.
- Female issues: PMS (premenstrual syndrome) and eclampsia.
- Psychiatric symptoms: irritability, depression, and bipolar disorders.
- Neurological symptoms: migraine headaches, excessive noise and pain sensitivity.
- Endocrine symptoms: insulin resistance.

The RDA for magnesium is about 2 mg per pound of body weight. The American diet typically provides 1.2 -1.5 mg per pound of body weight. Many magnesium experts believe that an intake range of 2.7- 4.5 mg per pound (about 400-700 mg a day) is optimal. Some on the forefront of magnesium research are recommending up to 1000 mg per day for healthy people, using the clinical symptom of diarrhea as a target marker. Once the marker is achieved, magnesium intake can be reduced. Asians, for example, are already taking 3-4.5 mg of magnesium per pound of body weight.

Caution: The above general recommendation for the *healthy* cannot be used for those with Adrenal Fatigue Syndrome. The diarrhea commonly experienced can be a welcome event for those with AFS and who are constipated. However, those with preexisting or borderline diarrhea (due to IBS and other conditions) may find their situation worsens. As nature's muscle relaxant, it also helps the body to relax under normal circumstances. In AFS, paradoxical reactions with magnesium are common, such as irritation, constipation, anxiety, and increased fatigue. As good as magnesium is, we must therefore be careful when using this nutrient for AFS.

Dosage Consideration: **400-1000 mg a day.**

Vitamin B Complex

The entire B complex is needed in small quantities to promote each other's functions, but it is also needed throughout the entire steroid synthesis pathway within the adrenal glands. Fortunately, only a small amount is needed, and most on a balanced diet will have no difficulty fulfilling this requirement. Food sources of the B vitamins include whole grains, brewer's yeast, and miso.

***Dosage Consideration*:** **Those who are nutritionally depleted can consider a daily B complex formula supplying at least 50-100 mg of B6, 100-300 mcg of B12, and 60-120 mg of B3.**

Trace Minerals

Trace minerals include manganese, selenium, chromium, iodine, copper, and zinc. We need these only in small amounts, and most of us received sufficient trace minerals in a balanced diet. Good natural sources of these trace minerals include sea vegetables, algae, and sprouts. We usually do not recommend taking a general trace mineral formula for Adrenal Fatigue Syndrome. Due to the body's sensitivity, many of these minerals tend to behave paradoxically. Instead of a general calming effect, zinc, iodine, and selenium in particular, can trigger anxiety for reasons not well understood. Prolonged intake of trace minerals is also generally not recommended because of their pro-oxidative effects.

In specific situations, individual minerals may be considered, and that usually is the best use of such trace minerals. For example, iodine may be considered for thyroid support, and chromium may be considered to stabilize blood sugar.

Dosage Consideration: Not recommended unless under guidance.

Quercetin

We can consider quercetin the king of flavonoids and an excellent natural antihistamine. It also interferes with the pain-promoting, inflammatory substances the body generates in many autoimmune diseases associated with AFS, including rheumatoid arthritis and colitis. This is of great importance in advanced Adrenal Fatigue Syndrome, where many suffer from food allergies, delayed food intolerance, and multiple chemical sensitivities. Having quercetin on hand can bring tremendous reduction of the inflammation triggered by allergens. Quercetin antihistaminic effect is non-sedating. That is, even if you take large amounts you won't become sleepy, which is a stark contrast to the drowsiness so common with over-the-counter antihistamine medications. Studies show that quercetin has the ability to fight off an enzyme that neutralizes cortisol, which as you recall, is a natural anti-inflammatory chemical the body produces.

We can get more quercetin by drinking unfermented green tea as well as red wine, but these foods are not recommended for those with AFS. Apples, onions, tomatoes, green peppers, and broccoli are excellent sources of quercetin. Since a large amount of quercetin is required to produce a positive effect, it's best to take it in supplements. Otherwise, most people miss the beneficial effect by not taking enough. Always take it along with the digestive enzyme, bromelain, for maximum effect.

Dosage Consideration: **600-6000mg per day (with bromelain) in divided doses on an empty stomach.**

Bromelain

The primary activity of bromelain, an enzyme found in pineapple stems, is to reduce inflammation and promote healing, especially in the muscles and joints. As such, it is used widely in sports medicine and trauma management. Bromelain's anti-inflammatory property also plays a significant role in managing asthma, arthritis, colitis, and other allergic responses. Use only high potency and high quality supplements. Bromelain works best when taken along with quercetin.

Dosage Consideration: **600-4000 mg. Bromelain's potency is rated in terms of GDU units; the higher the GDU number, the more potent it is. The recommended GDU**

units should be at least 2500-3500. We recommend taking bromelain on an empty stomach with quercetin.

Additional Gentle Nutritional Supplements

As we've said, the decision to take nutritional supplements in advanced AFS can be problematic because of potential paradoxical reactions. However, working with your doctor, consider taking the following in addition to those discussed in detail above. We employ these where specific supports are required and only when the body is ready. To achieve therapeutic effects, we need to ensure proper timing and dosage.

We suggest dosages, but these are subject to judgment and your doctor might want to adjust them to fit your needs.

- Vitamin D, 1000 to 5000 IU helps in hormonal synthesis.
- Lysine (an amino acid), 1-2 gm supports collagen synthesis.
- Proline (an amino acid), 500 mg-1gm supports collagen synthesis.
- Glutamine (an amino acid), 1-5 gm helps to stabilize blood sugar and the GI track.
- Chromium polynicotinate, 400-1200 mcg helps to stabilize blood sugar.
- SOD or superoxide dismutase, 100-1000 mg for liver detoxification.
- CoQ10, 300-1,000 mg, helps support cardiac heath especially if one has irregular heartbeat or is on statin medications.

- High potency fish oil, 1000-5000 mg DHA/EPA helps to support anti-inflammatory action.
- Chlorella, 1-2 tsp helps the body eliminate toxic metals as a natural chelating agent.
- Betaine hydrochloride (HCL), helps restore normal gastric pH if acid is deficient.
- Zinc, 25-50 mg can help support body metabolism.
- Malic acid, 50-200 mg helps enhance energy flow.
- Calcium D-Glucarate, 200-1000 mg helps liver detoxification.
- Activated charcoal as a gentle detoxifying agent and to combat diarrhea.
- Lithium orotate (a dietary supplement), 5-15 mg can help to stabilize mood swings.
- Gaba, 200-1500 mg can help reduce anxiety and promote better sleep.
- Taurine, 200-2000 mg helps with water retention by its natural diuretic effect.
- Soluble fiber, helps stabilize blood sugar and intestinal motility.
- Colostrum, 100-500 mg helps strengthen the immune system.
- Iodine, 3-50 mg helps support thyroid function if used carefully under guidance.
- Lipoic Acid, 300-600 mg a day by mouth or IV to support liver function.

Intolerance vs. Toxicity

While the nutrients discussed above are considered the most gentle, this is just a general rule of thumb. Remember that the more advanced the AFS, the more sensitive a person is to *any* nutrient. In addition, most compounds in this group are naturally occurring in our body from the day we are born. They are not foreign substances like herbs or prescription medications. As such, the body already possesses intrinsic pathways to absorb, assimilate, transport, and metabolize them. Overdoses produce only mild, if any, after effects and side effects. Symptoms of intolerance usually subside once supplementation is discontinued.

For example, excessive magnesium intake can cause diarrhea, which resolves after discontinuation. Fat soluble vitamins are more of a risk, but even with these, we now know that the upper safe limit is many more times than the Recommended Dietary Allowance (RDA). For example, the current RDA of vitamin D for adults is 600 IU; however, physicians routinely recommend 1000 IU a day. Some recommend up to 5000 IU a day, especially for those living in an area where sunlight is less abundant. The same is true for vitamin C. While the RDA is 60-95 mg daily, most healthy people take upwards of 1000 mg a day as part of a program designed to maintain health and prevent illness. The national nonprofit Vitamin C Foundation currently recommends 3000 mg a day for healthy individuals, and much more in times of illness.

The more advanced the AFS, the more challenging is the task to select the right compounds from this group. Invariably, those who are in very weak condition also have a highly sensitive body and are constitutionally weak. Some in this group can't tolerate any supplements. Others appear to get better at first, but then develop a gradual intolerance to these compounds and show more fatigue and anxiety.

With magnesium and vitamin C, for example, some individuals with AFS even develop constipation instead of diarrhea at high doses as the bowel tolerance level is reached. We see this as a paradoxical reaction. Well-being returns as the dosage is reduced.

While these kinds of reactions are reported as "vitamin toxicity," it should be more accurately described as a form of intolerance. The difference is significant. The body's unpleasant symptoms in such a situation are likely to be a reflection of its inability to clear metabolites out of the body and are unlikely due to the intrinsic toxic property of the vitamin or mineral itself. Reactions can be overcome by adjusting the nutrient dosage, and we often see intolerances resolve spontaneously as adrenal health returns.

Unfortunately, many simply abandon a good nutrient the moment such intolerance develops, labeling these valuable nutrients toxic, and forever depriving themselves of such treasured tools in the recovery process. This is very different from some compounds within Groups 2 and 3 (discussed in the next chapters) in which intrinsic negative properties exist that are true toxicities. The signs of toxicity appear at high dosages and compound the body's already poor clearance in those with advanced AFS.

We hope you see how important it is to match nutrient dosages to an individual's specific state. This is of paramount importance throughout the recovery process if a consistent and sustained recovery is desired, rather than a rollercoaster ride. Blindly taking supplements based on what works for others, an incomplete understanding of the intrinsic property of nutrients involved, and lack of correlation to one's unique constitution, can worsen AFS and trigger adrenal crashes.

Key Points to Remember

- Gentle nutrients include vitamins C, D, E, A, B5, pantethine, B12, chlorella, D-ribose, bromelain, quercetin, probiotics, collagen, enzymes, magnesium, HCl, phosphatidylserine, CoQ10, iodine, fish oil, and so forth.
- Vitamin C is particularly important, provided the right dosages, delivery systems, and forms are properly chosen and taken in a blend.
- Vitamin C is very safe, although caution should be taken for those with kidney disease, G6PD deficiency, kidney stones, and iron overload.
- Magnesium is an important mineral that relaxes muscles and calms the nervous system.
- Glutathione is an intracellular antioxidant and electron donor. It is the master recycler.
- Pantethine /pantothenic acid are powerful B vitamins with strong adrenal support properties in addition to their lipid support effect.
- D-ribose is a natural nutrient that enhances energy directly within the ATP cycle.
- Collagen is an important building block for protein needed for those in a catabolic state.

- Probiotics and enzymes are important tools to normalize internal dysbiosis (imbalance of intestinal flora) commonly seen when gastric assimilation slows down.
- Quercetin and bromelain are important natural antihistaminic compounds useful for those with chemical or food sensitivities.
- Intolerance to Group 1 nutrients should not be confused with toxicity.

Chapter 3

Second Line of Defense — Glandulars and Herbs

Glandulars and herbs have a role in a treatment plan for Adrenal Fatigue Syndrome. They can be considered when first line defenders described in the last chapter have failed to bring about complete recovery or in special situations. When we talk about *glandulars*, we're referring to raw glandular or non-glandular tissue derived from animals. Glandular products are commonly derived from several organs, including: thyroid, adrenal, thymus, testis, and ovary. Less frequently used are the pituitary, kidney, liver, pancreas, spleen, lung, heart, brain, uterus, and prostate.

Herbs are plants valued for their flavor, scent, or other qualities. Across our planet, they are universally used in cooking, as medicines, and often in spiritual rituals, too. Certain herbs can be beneficial for recovery from Adrenal Fatigue Syndrome, while other herbs can be quite detrimental and delay or prevent healing.

Both glandular products and herbs are widely used for Adrenal Fatigue Syndrome, but because of the lack of standardization and research, information about them is often incorrect, which tends to lead to their misuse. Proper guidance is needed in order to avoid the pitfalls and side effects.

Glandulars enjoy widespread popularity, and one reason is their adaptogenic properties, that is, their ability to enhance or boost energy when it's low and to tone down energy when excessive. These compounds are well suited for those with mild Adrenal Fatigue Syndrome, when the body has sufficient internal reserve. When adrenal function is compromised and has advanced to Stage 3C, the adaptogenic properties of many of these compounds become less apparent. Instead, for reasons not well understood, they tend to behave more like stimulants. This might be detrimental to those unaware and can lead to overstimulation of an already weak adrenal system. The more advanced the Adrenal Fatigue Syndrome, the more prominent the negative stimulatory effects appear. For this reason, what seems to be harmless for one person can be toxic to another.

The Basics of Glandulars

Past and current healers have frequently used tissue extracts to fight various diseases. This practice goes back over 3000 years. For instance, bone marrow extracts have been used for the treatment of anemia. Pancreatic glandular was standard therapy prior to the discovery of insulin. Desiccated thyroid is still used by many alternative practitioners to manage hypothyroidism. Many people use glandulars as a source of natural hormones. In addition, glandular therapy is the foundation for elements and components of today's hormone therapies, including thyroid and estrogen replacement, and steroids such as prednisone.

Commercial glandular extract therapy began in the 1920s with the discoveries made by Swiss physician, Paul Niehans, at his clinic in Montreaux, Switzerland. Dr. Niehans went on to develop live cell therapy, and thousands of severely ill patients came to his clinic as a last resort. His therapies also became famous for rejuvenation, and those who flocked to his clinic included the wealthy, royalty, presidents and celebrities. Live cell therapy remains a popular practice in Europe today.

By the mid 1930s, several companies produced *adrenal* cell extracts in liquid and tablet forms and countless physicians used them for their patients. By the early 1940s, adrenal glandular extracts were widely prescribed by physicians as part of their adrenal support treatment. As recently as 1968, they were still made by some of the leading pharmaceutical companies. Adrenal extracts are used to replenish and eventually normalize adrenal function. Adrenal cortical extracts can be discontinued once they have done their job of repairing adrenal function, which is their advantage over cortisol hormone replacement.

Theoretically, glandulars can come from any animal, but most often they are derived from cow (bovine), while others come from pig (porcine) and sheep (ovine). Different glandulars and glandular extracts have various properties and uses. For example:

- Thymus and spleen extracts may influence the immune system.
- Thyroid extracts can help with low thyroid.
- Adrenal extracts may help support weak adrenals.
- Testis extracts may influence androgen levels.
- Ovarian extracts may influence estrogen levels.

The difficulty of standardized testing prevents research and represents one of the primary setbacks in current use of glandulars. Modern scientific studies involve isolating variables into one variable used in double-blind experimental settings. Clearly, it isn't possible to test any glandular within the limited structure of a double-blind study because these substances contain enzymes, vitamins, fatty acids, amino acids, minerals, neurotransmitters, and a host of nutrients in addition to the tissues within the gland.

We can't isolate any single substance or hormone, such as cortisol or thyroxine, because of the many different substances present within each glandular extract.

Since glandular products contain many substances, including hormones, a major problem is our lack of knowledge about how much of these hormones or other substances are available in these extracts, which vary from batch to batch and animal to animal. In addition, it's difficult to know which of the many substances has a therapeutic influence and how the specific glandular interacts with myriad other substances in the body. With so many substances occurring in a single glandular, it's difficult to measure the kind of effect they may have in the long run, especially when used as a nutritional supplement. Nevertheless, based on eighty years of anecdotal evidence, little doubt remains that glandulars, when used properly, possess healing properties. Since the advent of adrenocorticotropic hormones, the use of glandular extract has been neglected.

Generally, the best glandular products come from freeze dried extracts derived from animals raised using organic methods in New Zealand, where no bovine spongiform encephalopathy (mad cow disease) has appeared. Reputable glandular products are subject to in-process and finished product testing. These tests include microbial contamination tests to assure acceptable total bacteria counts and the absence of disease-causing bacteria.

We consider each popular glandular individually.

Desiccated Thyroid Glandular

Desiccated thyroid is the dried and powdered thyroid gland, with the fat and connective tissue removed during processing. Desiccated thyroid is often derived from hogs, but may also come from cows and sheep. Desiccated natural thyroid is often prescribed to manage hypothyroidism. Pharmaceutical preparation is standardized and contains both thyroxine and triiodothyronine. Natural desiccated thyroid drugs have been available since the late 1800s, but fell out of favor in the 1950s when synthetic levothyroxine (Synthroid®) was introduced. However, the natural desiccated thyroid has regained popularity among patients and practitioners, in part because many patients report feeling better on these drugs. Armour® thyroid (porcine), and Thyrolar® (bovine) are common FDA approved drugs in this class.

Note: Prescription desiccated thyroid drugs are *not* the same as over-the-counter (OTC) thyroid glandular supplements. Countless OTC thyroid extracts are marketed as dietary supplements; many likely do not contain any significant hormones, but many do. Therefore, choosing the right product can become the proverbial tale of trial and error.

Many with Adrenal Fatigue Syndrome take prescription thyroid medication, making over-the-counter thyroid glandular unnecessary. Concurrent use of thyroid glandular and prescription thyroid replacement may lead to *hyper*thyroidism. If indeed the thyroid needs support, many other more gentle nutrients (such as kelp, iodine, and the amino acid, tyrosine) can be considered. Low thyroid function associated or secondary to Adrenal Fatigue Syndrome usually improves by itself once adrenal function improves.

Adrenal Glandular

Adrenal glandular products are widely promoted and used for Adrenal Fatigue Syndrome. After taking adrenal glandular, many users report that increased energy replaces fatigue and a sense of calm replaces anxiety. However, these reports generally come from those with *mild* AFS, not those with advanced adrenal weakness, in whom adrenal glandular often has a stimulating effect. As energy returns, this could be considered a desirable outcome, but significant side effects can occur if taken long term. *Taking adrenal glandular habitually to sustain energy is one of the common reasons for recovery failure, because these compounds can become addictive and produce withdrawal side effects when individuals stop taking them.*

Here's a closer look at how this generally unfolds:

- First, as seen with other addictive substances, the body can develop a tolerance and then more glandular is needed to produce the same effect.
- Second, at high doses, the glandular may actually trigger an adrenal crisis as the body's ability to handle the stimulant reaches maximum tolerance level. A wired-and-tired feeling may result in insomnia and hyperirritability along with extreme fatigue.
- Third, withdrawal and rebound symptoms may surface when the glandular is stopped, evidenced by even greater fatigue.
- Fourth, adrenal glandular may trigger a series of paradoxical and undesirable effects, including among other things, panic attacks, heart palpitations, fast heart rate, and fragile blood pressure.

Given these potential side effects, most consumers should exercise care and use adrenal glandular on a short term basis, provided that the Adrenal Fatigue Syndrome is mild. The more advanced the AFS, the more one should be wary of adrenal glandular and leave advice about its use to experienced clinicians.

Due to the lack of standardization, many products are available to consumers, but not all are created equal.

Other Glandular Products

- Thymus glandular contains substances that influence the immune system, but it is very difficult to know the nature of both their short term and long term effects on the immune system. The body contains countless immune substances, and it is extremely difficult to predict all the potential interactions when taking a thymus glandular. Furthermore, there could be wide variations in responses among individuals.
- Testis and ovary glandular extracts may contain testosterone and estrogen, respectively. Some consumers have tried to use these glandulars for libido support. We usually don't recommend them because much better ways exist to support and closely monitor hormonal function.
- Pituitary and hypothalamus glandular extracts are usually stimulatory in nature and should be used with caution. They are usually found as part of a scattershot approach to adrenal healing which is highly undesirable.

Taking a Look at Herbs

Every established civilization in the world has some form of herb-based tonic used to support energy. We now know many of these tonics support adrenal function through their main mechanism of action. The following herbs are commonly used for Adrenal Fatigue Syndrome recovery.

Licorice Root (*Glycyrrhiza glabra*)

Highly prized in Chinese medicine, licorice is grown in Europe and Asia and is used in many Chinese patented herbal formulas. The most well known herb for adrenal support, licorice is an anti-stress herb that increases energy, endurance, and vitality, and acts as a mild tonic. Licorice naturally fortifies cortisone levels by blocking conversion of cortisol into cortisone through inhibition of the enzyme 11beta-hydroxysteriod dehydrogenase. It has been used to help decrease symptoms of hypoglycemia, a common side effect of decreased adrenal function.

Licorice causes increased production of aldosterone, a hormone frequently deficient in advanced AFS. The herb can raise blood pressure for those whose blood pressure is normal. Although licorice candy doesn't offer the same benefits as preparations made from the root, it too, can cause an increase in blood pressure in those who are sensitive. Licorice can also soothe nervous stomachs and stimulate blood circulation in the heart. Until the 1930s, physicians prescribed licorice to treat Addison's disease.

Deglycyrrhized licorice (DGL) is made by removing the glycyrrhizin, the part of the plant responsible for its bittersweet taste. However, for positive adrenal effects, only real licorice should be used, not DGL.

Note: *Pregnant women should not take licorice. In high doses (3-5 gm/day), it lowers testosterone in women. Excessive intake can raise blood pressure.*

Side effects of licorice include headaches, elevated blood pressure (hypertension), lethargy, upset stomach, diarrhea, facial puffiness, edema, increased fatigue, anxiety, irritability, and grogginess. It may increase (potentiate) the effect of the drugs warfarin (an anticoagulant) and digoxin, a drug commonly used to treat cardiac disease. Here, as with glandulars, these side effects are more prominent in those with advanced Adrenal Fatigue Syndrome. The weaker the adrenals, the more we can anticipate stimulatory side effects. Most of the side effects are associated with what appears to be the loss of adaptogenic properties, which results in a preponderance of stimulatory properties.

Ashwagandha Root and Leaf (*Withania Somnifera*)

Ashwagandha is an ancient Indian herb with a history of therapeutic uses. Known as a tonic for all kinds of weaknesses, ashwagandha is famous for its direct beneficial effects on adrenal function. Ashwagandha promotes strength and vigor and is regarded as a rejuvenator and mild aphrodisiac.

Ayurvedic physicians use ashwagandha as the treatment of choice for rheumatic pains, joint inflammation, and other related conditions. Ashwagandha is also considered an adaptogen.

It is considered an adaptogenic, cardiotropic, and cardioprotective herb. Studies have shown that a 30-day course produces a significant increase in super oxide dismutase (SOD), an important antioxidant. Under a normal therapeutic dosage, patients do not experience side effects from ashwagandha. This means the herb is used no more than a few months, with intermittent days off or "holidays" if a high dose is used. To date, no significant drug interactions have been found. Some people have complained of slight drowsiness after using ashwagandha, but a majority of people have had no trouble at all, providing they are constitutionally strong.

Those with advanced AFS may find that this herbal compound increases energy. Like licorice, the stimulatory properties tend to be exaggerated and may become *too* pronounced in those with advanced adrenal weakness. This can lead to anxiety and a sense of being wired. For this reason, we recommend close monitoring if using this herb. However, for reasons we don't know, a small number of people with advanced AFS who have problems with other nutritional therapy may tolerate ashwagandha.

Korean Ginseng Root (*Panax ginseng*)

Generally, Panax ginseng enhances energy flow. It is more suitable for men than women, and some women have experienced adverse side effects, such as facial hair and acne. In men, taking too much ginseng can lead to symptoms of aggressiveness, irritability, or sexual excess. That said, Korean ginseng is a natural remedy for Adrenal Fatigue Syndrome and men can start taking it in small doses and gradually increase the amount. (It's best for women to avoid its use altogether.) Side effects include insomnia, headaches, upset stomach, breast pain, diarrhea, vertigo, and anxiety, and as with other herbs, its stimulatory properties tend to be more pronounced in individuals with weak adrenals.

Siberian Ginseng Root (*Eleutherococus senticosus*)

Unlike Korean ginseng, Siberian ginseng root is good for both men and women. The main benefits of Siberian ginseng are increased resistance to stress, normalized metabolism, and neurotransmitter regulation. Siberian ginseng counteracts mental fatigue and is known to increase and sustain energy levels, physical stamina, and endurance. In addition, Siberian ginseng is also an antidepressant that helps improve sleep, diminishes lethargy, reduces irritability, and induces a feeling of well-being. However, in the presence of AFS, Siberian ginseng root should be used short term and limited to mild cases in order to avoid stimulatory side effects that invariably overwhelm the body, and over time, worsen the overall condition.

Ginger Root (*Zingiber officinale*)

An adaptogen for the adrenals, ginger root helps modulate cortisol levels, normalize blood pressure and heart rate, burn fat, and increase energy and the metabolic rate. Ginger also stimulates digestive enzyme secretions for proteins and fatty acids.

Ginger root may contain aristolochic acid, which can cause serious kidney/ urinary system disease (e.g., renal fibrosis or urinary tract cancer). Symptoms include an unusual change in the amount of urine or the presence of blood in the urine. Liquid preparations that feature ginger often contain sugar and/or alcohol, so those with diabetes, alcohol dependence, or liver disease must be cautious.

Ginger is not recommended for use during pregnancy. Since it isn't known if ginger is excreted into breast milk, we recommend consulting your doctor before taking ginger root products while breastfeeding. (The casual use of small amounts of ginger as found in everyday cooking and baking or in commercial ginger teas is not detrimental.)

Ginkgo Leaf (*Ginkgo biloba*)

The ginkgo tree is one of the oldest living tree species, and ginkgo biloba comes from this tree. The Chinese have used ginkgo for thousands of years to treat various ailments, including lung congestion, asthma, to support circulation and libido, and as an anti-aging substance. It is well recognized for its positive effects on brain functions including enhanced mental alertness, reduced brain fog, enhanced memory, and reduced mental fatigue.

The adrenals suffer from a tremendous amount of oxidative stress, especially when producing excess cortisol during the stress response. This leads to a significant increase in free radicals within the same adrenal cells that make the needed hormones.

Ginkgo leaf possesses strong antioxidative properties to sequester free radical production, thereby protecting the adrenal glands, the brain, and the liver from free radical damage.

Ginkgo also contains several bioflavonoids that improve blood flow to the brain, ears, eyes, heart, and extremities. Its side effects include gastrointestinal discomfort, headache, increased risk of bleeding, diarrhea, nausea, vomiting, restlessness, anxiety, and increased fatigue.

Maca Root (*Lepidium meyenii*)

Maca root is an herb that grows high in the Andes mountains in South America at elevations up to 15,000 feet. It is one of the few plants that can be cultivated in the harsh climate of the Andes. For more than two thousand years, native Peruvians have used it as food and medicine, to promote endurance and improve energy, vitality, sexual virility and fertility. It is best known for its aphrodisiac properties. It also possesses adaptogenic qualities with glucose and cortisol. It has also been shown to reduce elevated glucose and stress-induced ulcers.

Active ingredients of maca root include free sugars, sterols, amino acids, alkaloids, tannins, and cardiotonic glycosidesuridine. The main physiological pathway of action is through stimulation of CNS, the central nervous system. Hormonal pathways do not appear to be involved. Studies show it does not influence hormonal blood levels of testosterone, for example. In addition to its aphrodisiac and energy boosting effects, this herb can also partially reverse sexual dysfunction that often occurs with the use of SSRI type antidepressants, such as Prozac®, Paxil®, and Zoloft®.

Being an herb of stimulatory nature, high doses can lead to anxiety and insomnia. Those with advanced Adrenal Fatigue

Syndrome are particularly vulnerable. Possible side effects include insomnia, anxiety, sense of impending doom, and nervousness. In extreme cases, one can develop irregular heart rate. For mild AFS, this herb is best used in small doses as part of a nutritional cocktail rather than as a standalone nutrient.

Rhodiola Rosea

Rhodiola Rosea is found in the colder climates of Europe, where for centuries it has been used to cure most ailments. Historically, rhodiola tea is popular among Russians as an energy booster. This herb can help ease the symptoms and support the healing process of many conditions, including anxiety, depression, stomach problems, fibromyalgia, and other nervous system maladies. This plant contains dozens of substances and it's difficult to identify all the active ingredients, although we can name rosavin, salidroside, rosin, and rosarin.

This herb is classified as an adaptogen. It acts as a muscle relaxant and regulates blood flow, which help support cortisol production in the adrenal glands when more cortisol is needed. It is better used in stressed individuals with high cortisol level during early stages of AFS. In some people, especially those in Stage 2 of AFS, the adrenal glands secrete too much cortisol. Unfortunately, the release is not steady but sporadic. Rhodiola rosea is also used to help the adrenal gland slow the secretion. This results in a sense of calmness throughout the day instead of periodic spikes of well-being followed by emotional lows resembling a rollercoaster ride. This herb can also help those suffering from fibromyalgia to sleep through the night and function normally throughout the day.

Rhodiola has also been shown to improve mental awareness, physical strength and endurance, stress, memory, and anxiety in healthy people. In the case of anxiety, it is best used when combined with other herbs such as kava, passion flower, 5-HTP, tryptophan, and ashwagandha.

In the presence of AFS, especially in advanced stages, it is important to remember that high dosages of rhodiola rosea extract could cause overstimulation and insomnia, thus aggravating anxiety and leading to a wired-and-tired state. On the other hand, those with mild AFS may find this herb an excellent adjunct in the early stages.

Caution: Herbs and glandulars are widely used and touted as possessing adaptogenic properties and marketed as tonics. Their stimulatory properties have made them popular among those with very mild AFS (who might not ever suspect they have it), because energy is increased and fatigue is reduced. Clinically, these stimulatory effects are more pronounced in those with weak adrenals. Stimulants are the equivalent of giving too much gas and flooding the engine in a car, thus putting additional stress on the adrenals to work harder and produce more energy. This finally further depletes the adrenal glands, and the short term sense of well-being tends to fail over time.

Short term use of herbal formulas and glandular products in mild cases of AFS is acceptable, but when adrenal weakness is pronounced, professional guidance should be considered. In addition, stay alert for the paradoxical or unusual reactions we have discussed elsewhere in this book, including:

- excessive fatigue
- panic attacks
- unstable blood pressure
- insomnia
- anxiety/irritability

Consider these warning signs of inappropriate use. Blended formulas are particularly convenient and effective, such as Adreno-Blast™ (see Appendix G). Glandulars and herbs have their place in adrenal recovery, and judicious use avoids over-stimulation, addiction, and withdrawal concerns.

Note: If you are already on high doses of herbs and glandulars, stopping abruptly can lead to withdrawal symptoms and may trigger adrenal crashes and is not recommended.

***Dosage Consideration*: Herbs and glandulars come in many forms, from raw powder to standardized extracts. Potency and purity also varies depending on the batch during harvest. It is not possible to give standard dosage recommendations. Always read the product label and consult your doctor prior to beginning such endeavors.**

Key Points to Remember

- Glandulars and herbs are widely promoted as healing agents for Adrenal Fatigue Syndrome.
- Many of these have adaptogenic properties and are useful in early stages of AFS.
- Their predominant properties tend to become stimulatory for those in advanced stages of AFS.
- Adrenal and thyroid glandulars from porcine (pigs) sources are the most common form of non-standardized glandular support.
- Popular herbs include licorice root, ashwagandha, ginger root, maca root, rhodiola rosea, ginkgo, and ginseng.
- Standardized thyroid glandulars are prescription medications due to their high potency.
- Due to the lack of standardization, it's not possible to recommend dosages for non-standardized herbs or glandulars; they are specific to each product.
- The use of glandulars or herbs, whether standardized or not, should be done with care and only as needed. Long term use requires professional supervision.
- Under most situations, this group is not needed provided that Group 1 compounds are properly used.

Chapter 4

Tools of Last Resort — Hormones

Adrenal hormones are essential for life and building and restoring health. Too much or too little threatens our well-being and prevents us living in optimal health. In the *early* days of adrenal hormone replacement, many decades ago, researchers had very little information about the proper dosage or the toxicity complications. Misled by improvement in their patients' symptoms, they gave patients many times more adrenal hormone, specifically, cortisol, than the normal amount. This sounds dramatic, but many patients died from the toxic effects.

Long term and excessive use of cortisol has negative side effects, too, so much so that cortisol is banned as a performance enhancing substance in competitive sports. Because of these bad experiences, researchers were scared off and avoided prescribing adrenal hormones such as cortisol whenever possible.

In Chapter 8, *Stage 3B—Hormonal Axis Imbalances,* we discussed the way some physicians use thyroid replacement to overcome the low energy brought on by Adrenal Fatigue Syndrome. This occurs because some practitioners assume patients with AFS suffer from primary hypothyroidism, and prescribe thyroid replacement. However, many individuals continue to suffer. Again, in the *early* days of thyroid hormone replacement, before synthetic hormones were available, patients received up to many times the usual dose of thyroid hormone, often resulting in severe toxic effects.

Clearly, hormone replacement therapy for AFS requires great care and its use must be put into perspective. In the right situation, with the right dose, hormone replacement can be of great benefit.

Medical science is just beginning to learn that even mild to moderate hormone deficiency, which remains undetected in routine blood tests, can nevertheless lead a person to feel awful and function poorly. We see this often in Adrenal Fatigue Syndrome.

To briefly review, adrenal hormones are under the control of the HPA axis, as well as the autonomic nervous system; over fifty hormones are involved. Dysregulation of any one can produce unpleasant symptoms. For example, low aldosterone levels can lead to blood pressure irregularities and fatigue; high estrogen can trigger PMS and anxiety; imbalanced cortisol output can lead to sugar dysregulation, hypoglycemia, and sluggishness; and high epinephrine output can trigger heart palpitations such as atrial fibrillation and panic attacks. Those in the advanced stages of Adrenal Fatigue Syndrome are especially vulnerable.

Since routine laboratory testing is often unreliable, we believe paying close attention to the signs and symptoms of AFS is perhaps the most effective way to assess the need for hormone replacement. Further, treatment decisions about hormone replacement for AFS are best left to knowledgeable, experienced professionals. Because we still lack complete understanding of these many hormones and their mechanisms, we always expect some trial and error, even in the best of hands.

Premature use of adrenal hormonal replacement is a common mistake and can be a major cause of recovery delay or failure. In fact, improper use of corticosteroid such as hydrocortisone can make the condition worse due to toxicity, paradoxical effects, addiction, and withdrawal complications. Worst of all, it may also trigger adrenal crashes.

Chapter 2, *Hormone Basic, and the "Forgotten" Adrenals*, also described the function of some major hormones, along with their potential role in treatment. We revisit these hormones from a therapeutic perspective now in order to see the way we use them as part of a recovery program.

Pregnenolone

Some AFS sufferers report that pregnenolone replacement improves their energy, vision, memory, mental clarity, well-being, and often libido as well. In addition, some women report fewer hot flashes or symptoms of PMS while on pregnenolone. This is likely attributable to the relative rise of progesterone and thus, reduction in estrogen dominance. Remember that pregnenolone is converted in the body to progesterone and these two hormones have some overlapping similarities.

The clinical picture isn't completely clear, however, because other women report that pregnenolone worsens existing fatigue and may even trigger adrenal crashes. Such paradoxical reactions are common, especially as adrenal weakness advances.

In addition, many can take what appears to be a normal dose, but they don't benefit if the body is shunting it towards cortisol production, a phenomenon known as *pregnenolone steal.* On the other hand, overdose is possible if too much is taken over time.

Pregnenolone is the chemical mother of DHEA, which in turn may convert into androstenedione, testosterone, and estrogen. Pregnenolone supplementation may increase other hormones in the body, particularly testosterone.

That said, the following guidelines are important:

- Typical starting dose is 15 mg, increasing up to 50 mg for men or women.
- Use pregnenolone derived from a pharmacologically pure product and not a yam-derived "precursor."
- Oral pregnenolone pills work well for most.
- Sublingual administration is a good option; it bypasses initial liver metabolism that occurs after swallowing an oral pill. Because of its fast delivery to the bloodstream it tends to be spiky and not well tolerated by those who are sensitive or in advanced stages of Adrenal Fatigue Syndrome.
- Low doses can promote a relaxed feeling, while higher amounts may lead to irritability. The exact reason for this is unknown.
- Acne and hair loss can occur, probably because pregnenolone is likely converted into androgens.
- Headaches are possible with high dosages.
- Irregular heart rhythm and heart palpitations can occur even when the dose is low. These side effects are potentially serious in the elderly or in those with heart rhythm disturbances.

Given these side effects, you can see why a healthcare professional should guide you and oversee the results. Do not rely solely on blood or saliva tests to determine how much pregnenolone you should take.

Note: Pregnenolone therapy may be contraindicated in some people with a history of seizures, because it may interfere with the action of medications used to treat epilepsy and depression.

Pregnenolone and DHEA (discussed below) can be taken together for Adrenal Fatigue Syndrome. Since some pregnenolone is converted into DHEA, the intake amount of DHEA can be lowered if both are taken together.

***Dosage Consideration:* 10-50 mg daily in divided doses.**

DHEA

The actions of DHEA tend to mimic pregnenolone, but are amplified, both in terms of desired results and side effects. Different doses appear to do different things, so we use DHEA judiciously.

DHEA converts into estrogen and testosterone. High dosages (100 to 200 mg or more) can lead to a redistribution of body mass as a result of the conversion of the DHEA into more androgenic steroid hormones. Significant side effects are similar to those of pregnenolone, only more severe. Hair loss and acne are particularly common.

For men, direct testosterone precursors such as androstenedione (and its metabolite androstenediol) may be more effective if anabolic results are desired. This, however, only applies to healthy individuals and not to those who are afflicted with Adrenal Fatigue Syndrome.

Even low dose DHEA can be problematic, because it tends to be quite stimulatory for those people with advanced adrenal weakness. In particular, those in Stage 3C and beyond (Adrenal Exhaustion) tend to react strongly even at minute dosages. Additional side effects are common and include: severe anxiety, feeling jittery, and increased PMS symptoms. These appear to be more prevalent in women.

Other important factors to consider include:

- DHEA is a slight mood elevator; it can potentially clash with antidepressants. Theoretically, antidepressant dosages can be lowered when the person is taking DHEA.
- DHEA has both a cholesterol lowering and blood thinning effect. Therefore, those taking cholesterol lowering drugs and blood thinning medications such as Coumadin® may need to have dosages lowered.
- DHEA is not regulated by a negative feedback loop in the body. In other words, taking DHEA supplements will not suppress the body's production of DHEA or cause the adrenals to rest and result in atrophy from disuse. Therefore, theoretically, patients do not need a resting period from DHEA, although it's probably good practice to have a resting cycle of a few weeks for each period of therapy lasting several months.
- Commercial DHEA products are made from *diosgenin*, an extract from the Mexican wild yam of the Dioscorea family. Biochemists can convert diosgenin to DHEA, but this happens only in the lab and not in the human body. Therefore, taking Dioscorea plant extracts does not lead to DHEA formation in the body.

Depending on the stage of AFS and individual constitution, both blood or saliva DHEA levels vary greatly as AFS progresses.

Because of inconsistent clinical correlation, blood levels generally are not particularly helpful.

> ***Dosage Consideration:*** **10-50 mg in divided doses. Use DHEA for Adrenal Fatigue Syndrome only under professional guidance. Determining the right dosage is not straightforward and can be tricky. The many possible side effects are similar to those of pregnenolone.**

Cortisol

Cortisol, by far the most important anti-stress hormone in the body, is produced in the adrenal cortex. It has a critical role in helping the body handle stress, including normalizing blood sugar levels and making sure the body has adequate energy to deal with the demands of stress. Cortisol also is a player in the body's powerful anti-inflammatory response, and it is a strong anti-inflammatory agent itself. (See Chapter 2, *Stress, Hormonal Basics and the "Forgotten" Adrenals*, for a detailed discussion of cortisol.)

Conventional physicians have been using cortisol, also known as *hydrocortisone*, to combat Addison's disease for decades. The drug is widely available under the trade name Cortef®. Some clinicians have advocated using cortisol to treat Adrenal Fatigue Syndrome as well. However, advances in nutritional therapeutics over the years have greatly reduced the need to use this medication in all but the most serious cases of AFS. We believe overuse of cortisol as an Adrenal Fatigue Syndrome recovery tool is a serious concern. On the other hand, cortisol can be a lifesaver for someone with severe adrenal weakness.

Prescribe with Care

Symptoms of intolerance are common in the more advanced cases of Adrenal Fatigue Syndrome. In other words, a good portion of people suffering from advanced Adrenal Fatigue Syndrome can't tolerate corticosteroid such as hydrocortisone. Their condition often becomes worse, even at low dosages. The exact pathophysiology is not known. Those who are severely decompensated are particularly vulnerable. Adrenal crashes may be triggered. Some patients require a few weeks to get used to the medication, and the beneficial effects may not be immediately evident. Still worse, we might have to deal with addiction and withdrawal symptoms. Anyone who has gone through that problem will tell you that most of the time the road is anything but smooth.

Fortunately, in most AFS cases, cortisol is unnecessary and is best considered a last resort. One of the key goals in AFS recovery is letting the body heal itself naturally. For those who have been on cortisol a long time, we support weaning off from it very slowly to break the dependency.

When cortisol is used, most patients find the following dosages effective:

- 5 to 10 mg in the morning
- Zero to 7 1/2 mg at noon
- Zero to 2 1/2 mg at 4 PM

This is a sample, and the actual dosage used by an individual must be adjusted to match the body's need. Some individuals do well on a morning dosage only, while others require an additional one to two doses each day. This should not be a long term recovery tool. If possible, those on cortisol should slowly decrease their dosage after a few months and eventually discontinue the treatment entirely. To avoid withdrawal side effects and adrenal crashes, we recommend first rebuilding adrenal reserves with natural compounds before titrating down cortisol dosage.

Many side effects of cortisol are possible and measures can be taken to counter them. For example:

- Shakiness can occur if the dose is too high, so lowering the dose is the solution.
- If patients experience an upset stomach, then they should take this steroid with meals. They can also lower the dose.
- If taken too late in the day, it can disrupt sleep.
- At a dose of over 20-30 mg a day, more toxic side effects of cortisol may start to appear. We don't recommend higher doses unless the benefits do clearly outweigh the risks.

For some, even proper cortisol replacement is inadequate or does not work. Remember that cortisol breaks the positive feedback loop between norepinephrine and CRH in the brain. If too little cortisol replacement is used, this effect will not be seen. On the other extreme, excessive cortisol can blunt adrenal cortex activity, leading to a reduced output of pregnenolone, DHEA, progesterone, testosterone, estrogen, and aldosterone. If this loss is large enough, calming signals from these hormones may be compromised. Norepinephrine and other anti-inflammatory responses may be dulled as well, leading to the opposite intended effect of cortisol treatment. This may explain why acceptance to cortisol therapy is not universally positive. In fact, some individuals feel worse while on the medication, reporting such things as increased brain fog, anxiety, and fatigue. At the same time, the autonomic nervous system (ANS) may put out more norepinephrine and epinephrine as a last ditch compensatory response, which contributes to a state of feeling wired-and-tired.

Cortisol mono-therapy (using cortisol alone) also does not work when AFS is accompanied by low blood pressure and electrolyte imbalance.

When Cortisol and Aldosterone Are Both Low

Cortisol and aldosterone can both become low, which usually happens in those who are already in Stage 3C and well on the way to Stage 3D, if not already there. Recall that aldosterone regulation is part of the renin-aldosterone hormonal axis system (RAS). In advanced AFS, low aldosterone can be the result of renin dysregulation, secondary to ANS imbalances, or as an independent event. Needless to say, the situation is dire. Extreme fatigue, low blood pressure, inability to stand for prolonged periods, orthostatic hypotension, and orthostatic tachycardia are the main clinical signs. In such cases, we consider the adrenal hormone, *fludrocortisones* (sold under the brand name Florinef® and available by prescription). This can be lifesaving because of its crucial salt regulation properties.

Florinef, also called 9α-fluorocortisol, is a synthetic corticosteroid with moderate glucocorticoid potency and much greater mineralocorticoid potency. It has been used in the treatment of cerebral salt wasting (extreme dehydration and low salt levels in the blood), where aldosterone levels need improvement. It is therefore commonly used in Addison's disease, the classic salt wasting (21-hydroxylase deficiency, an inherited disorder that affects the adrenal glands) form of congenital adrenal hyperplasia (a congenital condition in which the adrenals lack a necessary enzyme), and orthostatic intolerance. Side effects of this drug are extensive. They include edema, hypertension, headache, anxiety, hypokalemia (low potassium levels in the blood), worsening fatigue (especially at the start), increased sweating, hirsutism, peptic ulcer, insomnia, dyspepsia (generalized digestive problems), depression, and many more. Despite all the negatives, this is an important drug for those who have nowhere else to turn. This is truly a drug of last resort.

Unfortunately, many cannot tolerate Florinef, and a very slow and gradual build up is needed in the beginning. This is especially true for those who are very sensitive and constitutionally weak. The temptation is to rush into this drug too quickly, especially for those who are impatient and desperate to get well. While we do see good results with some, we must be reminded that some get worse because this drug can trigger further adrenal crashes. Close medical supervision is mandatory.

If blood pressure is pathologically low, we can consider adding anti-hypotensive agents such midodrine hydrocholoride (sold under brand names Proamantine® or Midodrine®). Side effects of Midodrine include high blood pressure, itching, numbness, and the feeling of writing on your skin or scalp. They tend to be transient. Both drugs are usually taken along with salt tablets or extra sea salt in the diet. Licorice also might help, but we use it with extreme caution for AFS because of its potential stimulating properties.

Dosage Considerations: **Florinef is available in 0.1 mg tablets. Typical daily doses for mineralocorticoid replacement are between 0.05 mg-0.2 mg. Start with half a pill in the morning for one week or two, and then go up to one pill in the morning if no side effects occur. Renin plasma, sodium, and potassium levels are checked**

through blood tests in order to verify that the correct dosage is reached. Midodrine comes in 5 mg pills. Starting dosage is one pill in the morning and one pill in the afternoon. Up to two pills three times a day may be needed.

Testosterone Replacement Therapy (TRT)

Testosterone is produced by both men and women, however, the amount women produce is much smaller and is produced in the adrenal glands. In both sexes, a decline in testosterone levels is associated with a decrease in sex drive and libido, symptoms many patients with AFS report.

In healthy people, testosterone replacement therapy (TRT) reenergizes the entire body, increases lean muscle mass, and reverses fat accumulation and muscular atrophy, which are normal manifestations of aging. Unfortunately, in AFS patients, TRT is not so simple. It does not work all the time, and aggressive use of testosterone can worsen AFS.

Testosterone helps to reduce norepinephrine and increase dopamine signaling in the brain. It also helps to reduce pro-inflammatory signaling. These are potentially good attributes. However, testosterone also suppresses ACTH and directly inhibits adrenal cortex activity. The net effect depends on the sum of all signaling interactions and that is hard to predict with any accuracy.

Low dose testosterone can be helpful in women. Men, on the other hand, require normal dose replacement if TRT is used at all. Low dose testosterone does not help men since it actually can suppress endogenous testosterone production, leading to increased fatigue. This is one reason why certain healthy men, even if hypogonadal (deficiencies in secondary sex characteristics) with low libido, cannot tolerate TRT. Those with advanced AFS are particularly susceptible to this type of unintended consequence. This is why we recommend optimizing the rest of the body's systems before considering TRT in AFS for both sexes. Pre-TRT workups should include a complete history and physical examination, together with a battery of blood tests including a male hormonal profile. In addition, we recommend cancer screening tests such as prostate specific antigen (PSA). These tests are necessary to rule out contraindications to TRT.

Testosterone replacement can have undesirable side effects, including frequent or persistent erections, nausea, vomiting, jaundice, and ankle swelling. Men may also develop breast enlargement because testosterone can be converted to estrogen by way of an enzyme known as aromatase. More serious complications include water retention, liver toxicity, cardiovascular disease, sleep apnea, and prostate enlargement.

Alternatives to testosterone include testosterone precursors, androstenedione and androstenediol. These are available in oral capsules or sublingual sprays.

Dosage Considerations: While testosterone replacement is one of the most effective ways to boost energy, this hormone should not be used in people with normal testosterone levels. In addition, testosterone replacement is seldom necessary in the treatment of Adrenal Fatigue Syndrome; many more gentle nutrients are available that do not expose the body to this strong androgen.

Estrogen and Progesterone

Reducing estrogen overload is an important clinical goal in recovering from advanced Adrenal Fatigue Syndrome. Direct application of natural progesterone is one way we can balance estrogen and progesterone. This also indirectly supports the adrenals by making more progesterone available as the precursor of cortisol production. Both go hand in hand. In addition, natural progesterone itself has a relaxing, calming, and sleep supporting effect which will further help to restore the stressed adrenals.

Conventional physicians sometimes prescribe *synthetic* progesterone (progestin) to combat estrogen dominance. This form is not the same as natural progesterone. Progestin is chemically *similar* to natural progesterone, but because it is molecularly different, its physiological actions are very different. Our bodies cannot convert progestin into cortisol to help the adrenals, or convert it to other hormonal compounds. However, *bio-identical* progesterone has this capability. In those suffering from advanced AFS, progestin can be highly toxic and hard to break down, which leads to a buildup of unwanted metabolites in the body. Therefore, the easiest way to restore balance to estrogen dominance is with *natural* progesterone.

Many delivery systems are available, but for most women, the low dose topical form is the most inexpensive and works well. The right time and dosage are keys to successful use, especially in the presence of AFS. Wrong dosage or timing can worsen AFS and could trigger adrenal crashes. Those in a low clearance state, characteristic of Adrenal Exhaustion, must be especially careful to correctly use progesterone, and in these cases even normal physiological doses may be too much for the body to handle.

There is great temptation to overcome estrogen dominance prematurely, especially if the clinical symptoms are severe. However, we believe it's best to any extent possible to heal the adrenals first and delay using natural progesterone until the body becomes ready. Many women can't tolerate progesterone if their adrenals are weak, because it taxes the liver, which metabolizes progesterone. As the body becomes stronger it is better able to tolerate natural progesterone.

Some controversy exists about the best delivery form of progesterone. Most physicians tend to favor the oral form (Prometrium), which is a prescription medication. A higher dose of the oral form is required, as compared to the cream form. This is the case because the oral form is assimilated in the gut and passes through the liver prior to being distributed to the rest of the body. This places an extra burden on the liver because it is the clearance center for this hormone. Since most with AFS are stressed and in a low clearance state to begin with, an overload of oral progesterone may trigger adrenal crashes because the liver is overwhelmed. However, this occurs subclinically, and liver function test results are usually normal.

Blood levels of progesterone tend to be short-lived, so women might need to split the total daily dose into two doses to achieve a more even or stable blood level throughout the twenty-four hour day. In short, we do not recommend the oral form of progesterone for those suffering from Adrenal Fatigue Syndrome.

Topical progesterone cream, which comes in a variety of concentrations, is the most common delivery form. For AFS patients the best option is the low dose over-the-counter (OTC) form. You simply need to apply 20mg of topical progesterone cream per day. Progesterone is lipophilic (dissolves in fatty substances) and it likes to stay in a fatty environment, allowing us to modulate the rate of release as follows:

- Application to an area such as the abdomen, which has a thick fatty layer, slows release.
- Application to an area such as the wrist, which has only a thin fatty layer leads to faster release.

Cream tends to be a bit messy, but for most in AFS, it is the best alternative overall, plus it's the least expensive. It's best to rotate the application site to allow the skin to refresh itself. Many OTC brands are available, but they vary greatly in quality.

Topical progesterone cream tends to release slowly over hours, days, or weeks from fatty tissue deposits. If used correctly, you can achieve a steadier blood level of progesterone with the cream than through any other practical method. Women suffering from AFS should be especially careful of compounded high potency progesterone cream, because it can trigger adrenal crashes. Even normal potency cream may sometimes be too much for those suffering from advanced Adrenal Fatigue Syndrome.

Side Effects of Natural Progesterone

Like most hormones, too much progesterone can cause problems. In the case of AFS, in addition to intolerance and sensitivity, too much progesterone is actually counterproductive. Consistently high doses of progesterone over many months eventually cause progesterone receptors to turn off, reducing its effectiveness. Furthermore, high doses may lead to toxic side effects, which can include:

- *An anesthetic effect such as slight sleepiness:* Excess progesterone down-regulates estrogen receptors, and the brain's responses to estrogen are needed for serotonin production. When this happens, simply reduce the dose until the sleepiness goes away.
- *Paradoxical estrogen dominance symptoms:* Some women report these for the first week or two after starting progesterone. After the initial application of progesterone, women who have been deficient in it for a period of years may experience some water retention, headaches, and swollen breasts. These are symptoms of estrogen dominance, but paradoxically they are

exhibited in the initial stages of progesterone application as the estrogen receptors are being resensitized by the progesterone and waking up. This usually goes away by itself and is not a sign of toxicity.

- *Edema (water retention):* This is likely to be caused by excess conversion to deoxycortisol, a mineralocorticoid made in the adrenal glands that causes water retention.
- *Candida:* Specifically, *Candida albicans* is a naturally occurring yeast that lives in moist areas of the body, i.e., the intestines and genitourinary tract. It's troublesome when it is out of balance with the other flora and immune system cells in the body. This imbalance can occur for many reasons. Oral contraceptives and antibiotics are often pointed to as culprits. Excess progesterone can inhibit anti-Candida white blood cells, which can lead to bloating and gas.
- *Lowered libido:* Excess progesterone blocks the conversion of testosterone to DHT. This primarily occurs in men.

Applying Progesterone Cream

The best low dose progesterone cream should contain 1.7 percent of progesterone and yield 20 mg of progesterone per application. The simplest application method is a metered pump that measures the exact daily physiological amount (20 mg) each time the pump is pressed. Progesterone is best absorbed where the skin is relatively thin and well supplied with capillary blood flow, such as the face, neck, upper chest, and inner arms.

For maximum absorption, spread on as big an area as possible and allow as much time as possible for absorption. If you're applying it once a day, bedtime application is likely the most convenient. Twice a day application is actually best, but it may prove troublesome for some. In addition, for either once- or twice-daily application, rotate to different areas of the body to avoid saturation in any one particular site.

Here is a sample rotational application protocol for twice a day application:

- Day 1 morning: Apply to the right side of the back of the neck.
- Day 1 before bed: Apply to the left side of the back of the neck.
- Day 2 morning: Apply to the right wrist area, with palm facing up.
- Day 2 before bed: Apply to the left wrist area, with palm facing up.
- Day 3 morning: Apply to the underside of the right upper arm.
- Day 3 before bed: Apply to the underside of the left upper arm.

Repeat this cycle from day 4 onwards. In other words, day 4 will be the same as day 1, and day 5 will be the same as day 2, and so forth.

Practically speaking, the best gauge for the ideal dose should not be determined by laboratory tests alone. When figuring out the ideal dose, symptom relief is the best gauge. In other words, *the right dose is the dose that works.* This is especially critical in Adrenal Fatigue Syndrome.

Always start progesterone only after the adrenal functional reserve is well established. When in doubt, start with a small dose, only under professional guidance, and slowly scale up if deemed beneficial.

The following are *general recommendations* for a topical progesterone cream application schedule based on a normal physiological dose:

- **Women in pre-menopause, still ovulating:**
  Those taking no hormonal supplementation: Count the day the period begins as the first day. Apply 20mg of natural progesterone every day from day 12 to day 26. Those with longer cycles may wish to start from day 10 to day 28. Begin the cream after ovulation, usually occurring 10 to 12 days after your period begins. If bleeding starts before day 26, stop applying the progesterone cream and start counting up to day 12, and start again.

- **Women in perimenopause (still menstruating with menopausal symptoms and/or PMS but not ovulating):**
  Count the day the period begins as the first day. Apply 20 mg of natural progesterone from day 7 to day 27. If your period begins early, stop using progesterone cream while you are bleeding.

- **Women in menopause (not menstruating):**
  For those not on estrogen replacement therapy: Choose a calendar day, such as the first day of the month. Apply 20 mg of natural progesterone daily from day 1 to day 25. Let the body rest for the remainder of the month.

If a woman has not been taking progesterone for a number of years, body fat progesterone is probably low. In this case, double up on the application for the first two months, and return to a normal physiological dose thereafter. Those who are already on hormonal replacement therapy with estrogen should also be on natural progesterone. Dosage varies depending on the given individual.

Using Estrogen for AFS: A Complex Issue

Some physicians advocate using estrogen (synthetic or bio-identical) for AFS. However, they might be misled into thinking estrogen replacement is needed, along with testosterone, because they see an initial increase in energy when hormone replacement drugs are prescribed. Estrogen helps generate energy, motivation, drive, competitiveness, and libido; it is also important for neuron growth and enhances memory. Because of its ability to improve testosterone sensitivity, it is not unusual for physicians to prescribe estrogen and testosterone together.

Estrogen has monoamine oxidase inhibitor (MAO) type properties, meaning it potentially has antidepressant effects. It also enhances serotonin receptivity in the female brain. The result is an increase in the neurotransmitters, serotonin, norepinephrine, and to a smaller extend, dopamine. When serotonin levels are adequate, we see that release of norepinephrine, an excitatory neurotransmitter, is inhibited in the brain. The results: estrogen helps control norepinephrine.

When serotonin cannot be taken up by the receptor site, because the site is deficient in estrogen, one can become irritable, fatigued, and anxious. However, excess estrogen can be pro-inflammatory, which reduces free thyroid hormone. This in turn can lead to a compensatory response of increasing norepinephrine with simultaneous activation of adrenal cortex signals through the HPA axis.

Excessive estrogen can have a destabilizing effect.

Because of this, prolonged estrogen replacement may lead to HPA axis dysregulation. As far as fatigue is concerned, it is not unusual to see those on estrogen replacement (with or without testosterone) do well at first, only to get worse as time goes on. Those with advanced AFS are particularly at risk for this outcome. Estrogen replacement therapy is therefore a complex endeavor with many risks that can lead to bad outcomes.

Fortunately, we find that estrogen replacement is seldom needed for those with AFS. Most are in the opposite state of excessive estrogen, or estrogen dominance, making the primary goal to reduce estrogen, not increase it. We do find, however, that small amounts of estrogen may be needed in those who have clear signs of estrogen deficiency, even though they have symptoms of estrogen dominance. Generally, these are underweight women whose fatigue is worse from day 4-14 of their menstrual cycles. These women should be on the alert for estrogen deficiency. We aren't sure why this occurs, but it may involve dysfunction in estrogen transport or receptor sites.

Most of the time, normalizing estrogen in AFS means reducing estrogen dominance through the use of natural progesterone. Proper timing is the key. Because estrogen is metabolized by the liver, the majority of those with advanced AFS will concurrently have weak liver function and slow clearance. Aggressively using estrogen before the liver and adrenals are normalized can worsen the condition and trigger adrenal crashes. Once a woman's adrenal function is stabilized, estrogen replacement can be of great relief if it's needed. Like testosterone replacement therapy, prior optimization of the rest of the system is the key to success.

Note: Because estrogen deficiency or dominance can produce similar symptoms, estrogen replacement, whether it is natural or synthetic, needs to proceed with care. For a detailed discussion on the proper use of estrogen, we suggest you read our mini-book *Estrogen Dominance* available separately as part of the Dr.Lam's Adrenal Recovery Series on our website.

Key Points to Remember

- Hormones commonly used for Adrenal Fatigue Syndrome include pregnenolone, DHEA, cortisol, progesterone, and testosterone.
- Premature use of steroidal hormones is a common recovery mistake and can worsen Adrenal Fatigue Syndrome.
- Compared to cortisol, pregnenolone and DHEA are both gentle hormones, but expect side effects in high doses or among those who are sensitive.
- Hydrocortisone is the most common steroid hormone prescribed. It should be considered as a last resort and for a limited amount of time, with an exit strategy well in place. We see potential addiction and withdrawal problems in addition to the many well known side effects at high doses or with prolong use.

- Estrogen and testosterone are normally not needed and have a limited place in AFS recovery.
- Estrogen and progesterone are important tools to balance female hormones, but to avoid taxing the liver and potentially worsening Adrenal Fatigue Syndrome, their use should be delayed until the adrenals are well healed.

Appendix A

Defining Our Terms

Throughout *Adrenal Fatigue Syndrome*, you will come upon certain terms and words that might or might not be familiar to you. Some terms come up in the text frequently, while others appear only once or twice. Rather than include a glossary at the end of the book, we decided to use this chapter to offer some easy, working definitions of commonly used terms. That way you can refresh your memory as they appear within the book. For example, throughout the text we refer to the components of the body's nervous system, and the definitions below will serve as a convenient reference. In other cases, we've defined terms we didn't define thoroughly when first seen in the text because they were used less often and we didn't want to stop the flow of information. Therefore, we added them to the list below. We also combined definitions of terms that logically fit together, rather than maintaining a strict glossary-style alphabetical order.

Acute/Chronic: When symptoms appear suddenly, we consider it an ***acute*** condition. For example, some common infections, such as colds, influenza, and pneumonia, come on quickly. The symptoms run their course and disappear as the body heals. Anaphylaxis shock is an acute allergic reaction to an allergen, and may be a life-threatening episode in an allergy considered to be ***chronic***, that is, an ongoing condition. Many conditions have both acute and chronic components.

Diabetes is a chronic condition with long term implications, but acute episodes of blood sugar/insulin dysregulation can bring on symptoms, such as fainting or severe weakness, serious enough to require emergency room visits. Rheumatoid arthritis and cardiovascular disease have both acute and chronic components. Avoiding acute episodes is one goal of managing chronic diseases.

Adaptogen: The ability to modulate and adjust to conditions as they change, whether or not these conditions are optimal. In the context of herbs, the term usually refers to the ability to bring the biochemical function back to normal, no matter if it is too high or too low.

Anabolic/Catabolic: Anabolic—The buildup phase of metabolism, in that our tissues are synthesized from the proteins and other substances we provide. ***Catabolic***—The breakdown phase of metabolism, in which the body supplies energy from the materials we have provided.

Autoimmune disorders: Many conditions, from rheumatoid arthritis to lupus to common allergies, result from the body's complex immune system. This system normally reacts to and works toward eradicating substances it perceives as "invaders." An autoimmune response occurs when the normal response is interrupted or disturbed and the immune system reacts to the body's tissues as invaders.

Challenge: Specific tests or protocols designed to prove or disprove a hypothesis.

Clearance: A measure of kidney and liver function. This refers to clearing a unit of a specific compound from a specific volume of plasma. The lower the clearance, the more compromised the function.

Crash: An abrupt state of reduced energy output and severe fatigue as the body reverts back to a simplistic form of function to conserve existing energy.

Decompensation: In medicine, when a previously working organ system or structure deteriorates, we call this decompensation. It can occur because of illness, stress, or aging. *Compensating* means the organ still tries to function despite the stressors. As Adrenal Fatigue Syndrome advances, the adrenals and other organ systems eventually begin to decompensate, potentially bringing on many confusing symptoms and organ system disorders.

Dysfunction: Impairment of a physiological function.

Dysregulation: Impairment of a physiological regulatory mechanism.

Metabolism: The overall term for the physical and chemical processes by which we produce, maintain, or breakdown the body's material substances.

Metabolites: The byproducts or results of metabolism. In addition, a metabolite is a product of metabolism that is more or less toxic to the organism producing it.

The nervous system: The central nervous system (CNS)—The portion of the nervous system that consists of the brain and spinal cord. The CNS gathers, stores, and controls information and is involved in all bodily and psychological functions, from breathing and walking to experiencing sadness and joy. ***The peripheral nervous system***—Consists of nerves and ganglia outside the CNS. It is divided into two parts: the somatic nervous system, which regulates musculoskeletal functions that help us deal with the outside world, and the ***autonomic nervous system***

(ANS), which regulates functions of the smooth muscles and glands within the body as described below.

Autonomic nervous system (ANS): The component of the nervous system that regulates involuntary actions, meaning we don't consciously control them, including heart and glandular activity. Multiple branches exist, the key ones being the **sympathetic nervous system (SNS),** the **parasympathetic nervous system (PNS),** and the **adrenomedullary hormonal system (AHS).**

Recovery cycle: When pertaining to Adrenal Fatigue Syndrome, recovery is the period immediately following a crash. Individuals will likely experience many cycles as they recover.

Stress: Put simply, stress is an individual's response to physical challenges, exertion, and events that create internal emotional pressure. We sometimes refer to the external events or circumstances as stressors, but our reactions are the source of stress, not the event itself.

Subclinical: Some conditions stay below the threshold at which we can detect and measure clinical signs and symptoms. For example, diabetes, hypertension, and hypothyroidism often produce symptoms, but clinical tests often show results in the normal range. We refer to this as a subclinical state. However, if left unattended, the condition can eventually worsen and abnormalities can appear on tests, hence, providing *clinical* evidence of their presence.

Unfortunately, subclinical states often occur but are ignored because the conditions are allowed to advance untreated until testing "proves" that the symptoms are real. In Adrenal Fatigue Syndrome, current testing techniques may produce results that look like there is normal adrenal function all the way up to adrenal failure. Therefore, we don't recommend relying on lab results as the final answer in diagnosing complex medical conditions and, in particular, AFS.

We hope these definitions will help you get the most from this book. Now, we begin discussing other issues related to AFS, as well as the stages of Adrenal Fatigue Syndrome.

Appendix B

Finding the Right Practitioner

The right healthcare practitioner can change your life. In the case of Adrenal Fatigue Syndrome, this is usually the most critical piece of the puzzle. Why? Because the vast majority of those with AFS experience myriad convoluted symptoms that confuse all but the most astute clinicians trained in this condition. It's essential to know what each symptom means, along with its significance. As you can see from the case studies, the right professional guidance can mean the difference between successful recovery and persistent failure.

Due to the general lack of Adrenal Fatigue Syndrome expertise among conventional and even alternative health practitioners, finding the right practitioner is easier said than done. Those with advanced Adrenal Fatigue Syndrome face the greatest challenges, as many have already been abandoned by conventional medicine and left to self-navigate.

It's worth spending the time to find the right clinician. Generally speaking, he or she should be an open minded and nutritionally oriented health professional. Additional clinical experience in endocrinology, cardiology, psychiatry, and neurology is beneficial, along with knowledge of using natural compounds in a holistic setting.

Insist on someone who can individualize your care, and look for someone who can examine diagnostic tests but also see beyond them to discern how you feel. Seek the clinician who believes that managing your adrenals requires a comprehensive approach, including modifying your diet, lifestyle, and exercise; this person's approach to natural compounds is both gentle and systematic and non-stimulating. Remember that a wrong approach can worsen your condition over time. In today's managed care and specialized environment, this is not an easy task, but neither is it impossible.

The Doctor Interview

You are entitled to ask a doctor key questions before making an initial appointment, and then based on the answers, ask yourself if this person is receptive to new ideas. What is his or her philosophy on how stress can affect the body? This will give you clues as to whether this doctor is holistic or conventional.

Later, when you talk with this doctor, does he or she clearly communicate the reasons you feel the way you do? An experienced doctor will generally have little problem tying in your various symptoms and giving you a comprehensive explanation. You should be able to receive direct answers to your questions in a way you can understand. This is part of being patient-oriented.

You can also ask about the doctor's philosophy of the adrenal glands as a key to the body's overall well-being and your symptoms of fatigue, along with other organ systems associated with your complaints, during the investigation. These questions help you indirectly gauge not only the doctor's knowledge of the adrenal system, but the more subtle understanding of adrenal function and Adrenal Fatigue Syndrome.

How to Best Communicate With Your Doctor

A good relationship is a two-way street, so the more clearly you communicate your problems, the easier it is for the doctor to address the issues. Here are simple tips to facilitate good communication:

- Have confidence in yourself, but do not show either an overly aggressive or passive attitude.
- Keep a journal of your health-related events and symptoms, noting when they come on (time of day or relating to an event or the menstrual cycle, for example), how they affect you, how you feel, and how and when you recover.
- Write down questions ahead of your appointment, so you can ask good questions and make the most of your appointment time.
- Trust your instincts. Your body is always right. Persist in finding the care you deserve. Don't settle for less.

Although we realize many doctors do not welcome patient-generated research, and some even become annoyed when patients bring them information, we recommend that you help your doctor stay informed. Print out articles relevant to your condition that you believe may help your doctor understand your situation, and submit these to your doctor for perusal ahead of time. Our Adrenal Fatigue Center at *www.DrLam.com* contains numerous articles that we constantly update. You can direct your doctor to our website. Forward thinking doctors, the real visionaries, thank us for providing this information online so they can learn and better serve their patients.

You have also benefitted from this book and other articles. You can better explain and describe your symptoms when you know more about your body and various conditions. This in turn helps your doctor help you.

If your doctor does not understand or cannot explain to you what is happening with clear confidence, chances are you need to consider finding another healthcare professional.

Investigate Other Options

Here are several tips if you cannot find the right practitioner:

- Connect with others who've had similar symptoms and investigate what they did to overcome their dysfunction. Do be careful not to draw conclusions too quickly, however. What works for one person may not work for another. You may be able to find a doctor through those who have been helped.
- Use the Internet. Search Adrenal Fatigue Syndrome and study relevant sites. Focus on educational sites that offer scientifically based information. Our site *www.DrLam.com* is a public educational website that contains the most easily searchable complete library of material on Adrenal Fatigue Syndrome on the web. Many articles on Adrenal Fatigue Syndrome not present in this book are available online, along with the latest news, FAQs (frequently asked questions), and an archive of questions many have asked through the years. You'll also find video and audio presentations of lectures on Adrenal Fatigue Syndrome. Those who like to be kept up to date on the latest news on this topic can sign up for our free electronic newsletter.
- Be wary of Internet forums because views expressed are often skewed and not objective in nature. What works for one person can in fact be toxic for another. Be skeptical of anyone who purports to have simple, quick fix or break-through solutions. Watch out for those who post angry

messages or who are overly active online. These individuals may have hidden agendas or unresolved psychological or undisclosed physical issues well beyond AFS. Finally, be careful of one-size-fits-all approaches; these seldom work except for the mildest cases.

- If you are not sure whether you have Adrenal Fatigue Syndrome, or if you would like an assessment on the degree of your adrenal function, take our Three Minute Test in this book (Appendix F) or online at *www.DrLam.com.*
- If you have specific questions about your symptoms or condition, write to us directly from our website at *www.DrLam.com.* Each question is individually answered privately and in confidence.

Fortunately, travelling is not usually required in order to seek help. We serve clients all over the world. If you cannot find a practitioner with whom you are comfortable, or if you have no one to turn to, call us. (For details see our website.)

Our telephone-based nutritional coaching program is an individualized one-on-one program designed to facilitate the fastest possible recovery using natural measures. It incorporates many principles and techniques discussed in this book.

Appendix C

Liposomal Encapsulation Technology

In existence since the early 1970s, liposomal encapsulation technology (LET) is the newest delivery method used by medical researchers to transfer drugs that act as healing promoters to specific organs. In other words, LET offers targeted delivery of vital compounds to the body. The excellent transference capability of LET has led some manufacturers to use it in their topical moisturizers and other cosmetic products.

The astounding effects and advantages derived from LET are the reason that a number of nutritional companies use this technique in the oral delivery of dietary supplements.

The advantage of LET is its ability to carry power packed and non-decomposed natural compounds to pinpointed tissues and organs. Even if doses are 5 to 15 times less than normal supplemental intake, the delivery system's effectiveness remains unchanged. This reduction is both medically and economically significant.

Tablets, capsules, and topical nutritional products are affected by environmental conditions such as moisture, oxygen, and other unfavorable factors. For example, nutrients are likely degraded by enzymes and esophageal digestive juices prior to being absorbed into the body. In addition, binders, fillers, gelatins, and sugar are food additives that affect the absorption process. This partial assimilation caused by the incomplete disintegration of the tablet or capsule is a serious problem. LET shields substances from these negative properties, which are likely to take place within the gastrointestinal passage.

Liposomal encapsulation employs a phospholipid liposome (see the definition below) to construct a defense that repels the negative activities of the digestive juices, alkaline solutions, salts, and free radicals of the body. The duration of this protection lasts from the moment the nutrients are on their way toward the gastrointestinal tract, until the contents have reached the target tissue and are immediately taken in by the cellular structure and transferred into the intra-cellular space.

A majority of the liposomes in LET are composed of phospholipids. All bodily cells contain a protective membrane consisting of phospholipids. This substance is required by the body to grow and function.

Phospholipid Structure

Phospholipids are the main building blocks of cell membranes in the human body. The three major portions of the molecule consist of one head and two tails. The three molecular parts of the head are: glycerol, phosphate, and choline. The *hydrophilic* character of the head makes it captivating to water while the long tail is composed of saturated fatty acids. The *hydrophobic* trait of the fatty acids makes them repelled by water. The heads of the phospholipid line up side-by-side next to each other when placed in a water-based solution. Due to the hydrophobic tails, another phospholipid will line up tail-to-tail in response to this similar environment; they form an identical image of each other, thus making a natural environment of dual rows of closely packed phospholipid molecules called the *phospholipid bi-layer*. These bi-layers surround all the cells. The size of one bi-layer is equivalent to 1/1000th the thickness of one book page. Nutrients are ably directed in and out of the cells by different combinations of proteins found in the bi-layer of the phospholipid. Just imagine, we have 70 trillion cells in the body and 1,000 phospholipids are found in every single cell. Without the phospholipids, the body ceases to work properly because, as stated, they are the basic building blocks of the body. Various types of phospholipids are classified based on the type of fatty acids connected to the head of the choline phosphate.

The essential polysaturated fatty acids make *phosphatidylcholines (PC),* essential phospholipids. Liposomal capsules are created by using these PC fatty acid phospholipids. Phospholipids and PC are both essential to life and the body requires them.

Benefits of Phospholipids

We derive many benefits from phospholipids. The most essential is its astounding anti-aging effect. For example, phospholipids can decrease total serum lipid (fat) and LDL (the bad cholesterol), increase HDL (the good cholesterol), decrease triglyceride and platelet aggregation, amplify red blood cell fluidity, heighten coronary circulation, expand exercise tolerance, increase quality of memory, increase immunity, and improve liver protection and rejuvenation.

Countless research studies have been conducted on the benefits of phosphatidylcholine, and 500 human studies have proven that PC guards and improves the health of lipids.

Of all bodily organs, the liver performs the most essential activity. Nowadays, the liver is exposed to the highest level of toxic pollutants, such as gasoline, exhaust fumes, paint, pesticides, contaminated water, and many others. As the biggest organ, the liver is the front line of the body's defense against these toxins. The main work of body lipids is to detoxify and bring nourishment, including vitamins A, E, and D, and glycogen, to the whole body.

The liver absorbs and combines all the 100 essential enzymes needed for assimilating nutrients. The function of the liver is enormous: It filters one half gallon of blood every minute and every day it breaks down and detoxifies over 10,000 compounds like poisons, hormones, toxins, and enzymes. PC guards the liver from the toxins; every day, it takes 1000 to 2000 mg of PC to guard the liver from injuries just caused by alcohol. We also know that taking PC one day before exposure to radiation can protect the body against its harmful effects.

The heart, blood, and entire cardiovascular system are greatly improved by PC because of its ability to decrease LDL cholesterol and amplify HDL cholesterol. By taking in 1500 mg of PC every day for a month, studies show a 12-14percent increase of HDL ratio over the LDL ratio among diabetic patients. PC also lowers serum triglyceride and overall cholesterol levels, but the degree of reduction depends on the amount of the dosage and length of time it's taken. For example, we can see a 4.9 percent decrease in serum triglyceride after taking a 1500 mg PC dosage over a four week period. Taking in 3000 mg daily over an eight week period will reduce cholesterol by 44 percent. PC intake can bring about a maximum decrease in serum triglyceride, increase exercise tolerance, and improve cardiovascular system function.

Taking 1800 mg of PC daily for a month resulted in a significant improvement in the muscular and leg blood flow in a group of heart patients; these patients were able to walk, without any kind of chest pain, more than 100 times further by taking only PC.

PC protects cells in several ways. First, it lessens lipid peroxidation brought about by an increase in HDL and a decrease of serum lipid. (Peroxidation is a process that results in free radicals stealing electrons from the lipids in the membranes of the cells, thus causing cell damage.) Second, oxidized low-density lipids in cell membranes are replaced by PC. Third, oxidized cholesterol is eliminated by PC. PC conducts an overall cell repair of the lipid peroxidation. Several clinical instances have demonstrated the ability of PC to limit and prevent the reverse of the peroxidation process.

PC liposomes are the essential parts of LET and serve as the areas wherein the encapsulated supplements are delivered. Liposomes vary in size, which are determined by the process they were made. The measurement can range from hundreds of micrometers (one millionth of a meter) to under 100 nanometers (one billionth of a meter) and the structures are unilamellar (single layer), bilamellar (double layer), or mutlilamellar (multi layer). A variety of methods exist to prepare a liposome. To orally deliver nutrients, the main device is the mechanical method.

When categorizing the mechanical preparation process, we have three major classifications: extrusion, micro-fluidization, and sonification. The maximum state of liposomal technology should use a liposome below 200 nanometers with a bi-layer structure and phosphatidylcholine. Eggs and soy are the most common sources and must be stored at room temperature above freezing.

LET at Work

Glutathione and vitamin C represent an excellent example of LET's application. A majority of animals produce vitamin C in their livers and kidneys. The exceptions include humans, apes, and guinea pigs. Goats produce as much as 13,000 milligrams of vitamin C in a day, but can exceed 100,000 milligrams in the presence of pathogens and toxins.

In its traditional form, oral vitamin C had a slow rate of assimilation at high dose, yet vitamin C is called the super-antioxidant because of its ability to neutralize free radicals. If a high dosage is needed, it is advisable to take vitamin C intravenously because of superior blood and tissue absorption. When taken by mouth in high dose, only 10-15 percent of high dose vitamin C is absorbed. Using LET technology has greatly improved and updated the transfer of vitamin C into the cells, making it by far the best way for vitamin C to enter the hepatic (pertaining to the liver) system in its pure condition.

Vitamin C is guarded by PC liposomes from injury done by the enzyme and gastric juices in the digestive system. Once they enter the body, PC liposomes pass through the small intestine smoothly without expending any energy. The liposomes are carried by the system to the liver in complete form and are prepared to give off their content. The PC liposomes in the liver are scattered. The polyunsaturated PC is ingested by the liver cells as it frees the encapsulated vitamin C.

Common side effects of oral vitamin C (powder, capsule, and tablet forms) include diarrhea and gastric discomfort. Oral liposomal encapsulated vitamin C increases the supply of vitamin C into the cellular system much more effectively and without negative effects such as gastric distress, and extra load on the liver.

While liposomal encapsulation technology represents an excellent delivery system, it is important to note that normal routes of delivery (such as tablets, capsules, and powder forms) are still useful in that they offer different and complimentary forms of nutrient bioavailability to ensure a steady blood level throughout the day as desired.

Designing a comprehensive program combining various forms of delivery systems to ensure consistent nutrient delivery throughout the day requires extensive clinical experience. If done properly, one can see dramatic clinical results, and this is a hallmark of clinical excellence.

Several reputable brands are currently available on the market. LipoNano® C comes in a liquid form and offers a high potency form of liposomalized vitamin C. More vitamin C per unit dose means less has to be taken to get the same effect. Make sure you read the label carefully. Avoid products that contain alcohol which is taxing on the liver and, therefore, not recommended. Those in advanced AFS or who have compromised liver clearance are particularly vulnerable.

A Word about Preservatives

Preservatives are used in most liquid nutritional formulas. They serve to increase the shelf life of a product by preventing (or delaying, at least) spoiling. Commonly used preservatives include sodium benzoate, potassium sorbate and alcohol. Alcohol in particular has been long used by the pharmaceutical industry as a solvent, penetration-enhancer, disinfectant and preservative. A 7 to 12 percent alcohol content is commonly used in many skin-care products, a concentration that can be significantly toxic to skin cells. The skin, like liver, is one of the few organs capable of metabolizing alcohol to another cytotoxic chemical acetaldehyde.

In the case of advanced AFS, where liver function is often compromised at the subclinical level, intake of alcohol from such a preservative only adds further burden to the already weak and low clearance capability of the liver. Alcohol may therefore deter the healing process, and in extreme cases, precipitate adrenal crashes. Look for formulas that are non-alcoholic and have as little preservatives as possible.

Appendix D

Suggested Reading and Resources on the Adrenal Fatigue Syndrome

In addition to the books, CDs and DVDs listed in the front of *Adrenal Fatigue Syndrome*, here are additional free readings and resources from our website, *www.DrLam.com/afs/*. When on the site, just click on the topic of interest. Each will help you understand the scientific basis of our approach to Adrenal Fatigue Syndrome we take throughout this book.

Acidosis
Aging Brain
Andropause
Atrial Fibrillation
Beef, Chicken, or Fish
Blood Thinners and Nutritional Supplements
Chelation
Cholesterol
Dehydration
Detoxification
DHEA
Diabetes
Eggs—Good for your body?
Endometriosis
Nutritional Supplements—To Take or Not?
Omega 3 Fatty Acid
Oral Health
Progesterone
The Big Fat Lie
Estrogen Dominance
Fibroids
Heart Disease Prevention—A Complete Nutritional Approach
Hypothyroidism
Insulin and Aging:
Magnesium and Aging
Menopause
Metabolic Syndrome
Milk—The Perfect Food?
My Doctor Is Killing Me
New Markers of Cardiovascular Disease
Nutritional Medicine
Upper Limits Vitamin C and E Intake
Water
Where to Buy Supplements
Why Conventional Medicine Rejects Adrenal Fatigue Syndrome

After Recovery

After your recovery from Adrenal Fatigue Syndrome, the natural progression is to embark on an anti-aging program where you begin to reverse the biological clock naturally, while keeping AFS at bay. We have a complete library on this in our website. The following articles are helpful and found also on *www.DrLam.com/afs/.*

- Anti-aging Program
- Anti-aging Strategies
- Blood Type Diet
- Osteoporosis
- Woman's Optimal Daily Allowance
- Dr. Lam's Smoothie Recipe
- Customized Exercise Routine
- Links to Various Health Centers
- Calories That Count
- Men's Optimal Daily Allowance
- Links to Natural Protocols for Common Health Conditions

For the Avid Reader in Natural Health

You can download our free online ebooks from our home page at *www.DrLam.com:*

Beating Cancer with Natural Medicine

5 Proven Secrets to Longevity

Other Useful Links

New information and links on natural health and Adrenal Fatigue Syndrome are regularly added to our website library. These include many nonprofit educational organizations, links to scientific journals, periodicals, and additional recommended books.

Here is the link: *http://www.DrLam.com/links.asp*

Appendix E

3 Minute Adrenal Fatigue Syndrome Test

Here is a checklist of common symptoms associated with Adrenal Fatigue Syndrome. Check the boxes that are applicable. See your score below and find out what you can do about it.

- ❑ Tendency to gain weight especially at the waist and inability to lose it.
- ❑ High frequency of getting the flu and other respiratory diseases that tend to last longer than usual.
- ❑ Reduced sex drive.
- ❑ Lightheaded when rising from a supine position.
- ❑ Unable to remember things and unclear thinking.
- ❑ Lack of energy in the mornings and also in the afternoon between 3-5:00 PM.
- ❑ Feel better suddenly for a brief period after a meal.
- ❑ Need coffee or stimulants to get going in the morning.
- ❑ Crave for salty, fatty, and high protein food such as meat and cheese.

- ❑ Increased symptoms of PMS for women; periods are heavy and then stop, or almost stop on the 4th day, only to start to flow again on the 5th or 6th day.
- ❑ Pain in the upper back or neck for no apparent reasons.
- ❑ Easily startled.
- ❑ Decreased ability to handle stress and responsibilities.
- ❑ Body temperature is off balance; hands and feet feel cold, face feels warm, or hot flashes.
- ❑ Unexplained hair loss.
- ❑ Tendency to tremble when under pressure.
- ❑ Multiple allergies such as asthma, hay fever, skin rashes, eczema, hives, and food sensitivity.

Enter the number of checkmarks you have made: ______

What does your score mean?

If your score is 4 or below, chances are you do not have Adrenal Fatigue Syndrome unless your symptoms are quite severe. There may be other dysfunction in place. Adrenal Fatigue Syndrome is unlikely to be significantly involved, although we can't be sure without a detailed history. You can adopt many of the dietary and lifestyle recommendations in this book as they are generally conducive to good health. Group 1 and 2 nutritional supplementations (Chapters 20 and 21 in the book, *Adrenal*

Fatigue Syndrome) are generally well tolerated if your doctor approves. If you do not improve within a reasonable amount of time, write to us through our website with your score and what you did. We will give you our thoughts in confidence.

If your score is 5-9, you may or may not have Adrenal Fatigue Syndrome. Many conditions mimic AFS, so if you have not already done so, visit your doctor for further medical investigation. If you are given a clean bill of health but remain symptomatic, consider Adrenal Fatigue Syndrome. The higher your score on the test, the higher your risk of Adrenal Fatigue Syndrome. You also can adopt many of the dietary and lifestyle recommendations mentioned in this book, but be cautious when it comes to nutritional supplementation, as they can worsen the condition if not properly used. If you are not sure where you stand or what to do, then write directly and privately to us online through our website (*www.DrLam.com*) with your score and a brief history. We'll give you our assessment and suggestions in confidence.

If your score is 10 or above, it is imperative that you become fully educated about Adrenal Fatigue Syndrome and alert your doctor about this condition. The more severe your symptoms, the more dysfunctional your adrenal glands likely are. We *do not* recommend self-navigation as it often makes the condition worse over time. If you cannot find someone knowledgeable to help you, if you fail to improve on your recovery plan, and are not sure where you stand or what to do next, then write to us directly and privately through our website (*www.DrLam.com*). Let us know your score, a detailed medical history, and your main complaints. We will reply to you in confidence and give you some guidance.

This free test is also available online at our website *www.DrLam.com.*

Appendix F

Nutritional Supplement Blends for AFS

Not all supplements are created the same. Quality varies greatly, depending on ingredients and the manufacturing process. Inferior quality supplements can deter the recovery process and actually make things worse. Buying supplements based on price alone is a common recovery mistake.

To ensure the highest quality and consistency based on latest research, we have formulated our own line (Dr.Lam) of dietary supplements. They are made specifically for those with AFS and those who believe in using nutritionals to deter the aging process. Most people with AFS are highly sensitive. We have to be very careful about what we recommend. Knowing the exact blend and ingredients of each formulation gives us great insight and advantage on how to match each person's nutritional need with their body state during each step of their recovery. These products are made in the United States under strict manufacturing standards.

The complete line is available at *SupplementClinic.com*, the most complete online dietary supplement retailer dedicated to AFS, providing everything from supplements to books, video and saliva test kits. In addition to having reasonable price and excellent service, they ship worldwide. Royalties received go to support the ongoing mission of *DrLam.com*.

Some of the most popular of Dr. Lam's nutritional formulations designed for Adrenal Fatigue Syndrome are:

Quantamax®: Quantamax is a technologically advanced health drink formulated in a special matrix of mineral ascorbates, amino acids, co-factors, and immune-enhancing nutrients. This support provides the nutrients necessary to help rebuild and rejuvenate the important adrenal and cardiovascular collagen network in our bodies, leading to healthier adrenals, skin and decreased risk of cardiovascular disease. This blend formula provides for quick and gentle energy boosts without the over-stimulatory, spiky side-effect of ascorbic acid.

C-Support: C-Support is a cutting-edge blend of four different sources of Vitamin C including ascobyl palmitate, the fat soluable form. This formula provides a precise balanced ratio designed for sustained release to achieve optimal biological activity of Vitamin C in the body.

Pandrenal®: Pantethine, along with pantothenic Acid (Vitamin B5), forms a powerful blend in supporting adrenal glands and normal cholesterol levels in the body. Both are needed, and having the right ratio of each is important to harvest the synergistic effect. It is manufactured in a hermetically sealed soft-gel to deliver the purest and most potent combination possible.

Adreno-Blast™: The formula contains a blend of adrenal glandular, adaptogenic herbs, and four types of ascorbates designed to increase overall body energy, while decreasing exhaustion and fatigue. This is particularly useful for those in mild or recovering AFS when the body is stable.

LipoNano® C: LipoNano C represents a major breakthrough in the therapeutic nutrient delivery system of Vitamin C, with several key characteristics. First, Liposomal Encapsulation Technology (LET) is used. It combines nano-technology and bio-technology in a powerful way to take advantage of characteristics of liposomes similar to that made by Mother Nature, using natural ingredients such as essential fatty acids and phospholipids.

Second, these liposomes are naturally strong and sized perfectly for maximum stability during transport and easy penetration at the cellular level, just as Mother Nature intended. Third, the liposomes contain nutrients and synergistic co-factors in a micro-bubble. Cellular bioavailability is significantly enhanced. Due to the high potency of this formula, always start a with small amount.

LipoNano® Glutathione: Glutathione, an antioxidant produced by the body that fastens to and gets rid of toxins, is necessary to help purge the body of poisonous metabolic waste and to maintain the immune system. When exposed to aging and stress, our glutathione levels drop. Synergistic co-factors, such as Vitamin E and B12, are important elements that enhance clinical outcome. Replenishment is critical to enhance AFS recovery.

About the Authors

Michael Lam, M.D., M.P.H., A.B.A.A.M., is a western trained physician specializing in nutritional and anti-aging medicine. Dr. Lam received his Bachelor of Science degree from Oregon State University, and his Doctor of Medicine degree from the Loma Linda University School of Medicine in California. He also holds a Master's degree in Public Health. He is board certified by the American Board of Anti-Aging Medicine where he has also served as a board examiner. Dr. Lam is a pioneer in using nontoxic, natural compounds to promote the healing of many age-related degenerative conditions. He utilizes optimum blends of nutritional supplementation that manipulate food, vitamins, natural hormones, herbs, enzymes, and minerals into specific protocols to rejuvenate cellular function.

Dr. Lam was first to coin the term, *ovarian-adrenal-thyroid (OAT)* hormone axis, and to describe its imbalances. He was first to scientifically tie in Adrenal Fatigue Syndrome (AFS) as part of the overall neuroendocrine stress response continuum of the body. He systematized the clinical significance and coined the various phases of Adrenal Exhaustion. He has written four books: *The Five Proven Secrets to Longevity, Beating Cancer with Natural Medicine, How to Stay Young and Live Longer, and Estrogen Dominance.*

In 2001, Dr. Lam established *www.DrLam.com* as a free, educational website on evidence-based alternative medicine for the public and for health professionals. It featured the world's most comprehensive library on AFS. Provided free as a public service, he has answered countless questions through the website on alternative health and AFS. His personal, telephone-based nutritional coaching services have enabled many around the world to regain control of their health using natural therapies.

Dorine Lam, R.D., M.S., M.P.H., is a registered dietitian and holistic clinical nutritionist specializing in Adrenal Fatigue Syndrome and natural hormonal balancing. She received her Bachelor of Science degree in Dietetics, holds a Master's Degree in Public Health in Nutrition, and a Master of Science degree in Nutrition from Loma Linda University, in Loma Linda, California. She is also a board-certified, Anti-Aging Health Practitioner by the American Academy of Anti-Aging Medicine. She coauthored with Michael Lam, M.D., the book *Estrogen Dominance* and numerous articles on Adrenal Fatigue Syndrome. Her personal research and writing focuses on the metabolic aspect of Adrenal Fatigue Syndrome.

She is married to Michael Lam and is an integral part of the telephone-based nutritional coaching team helping people overcome Adrenal Fatigue Syndrome.

Printed in Great Britain
by Amazon